# Winning With Quality:
## The FPL Story

# Winning With Quality:
## The FPL Story

## John J. Hudiburg

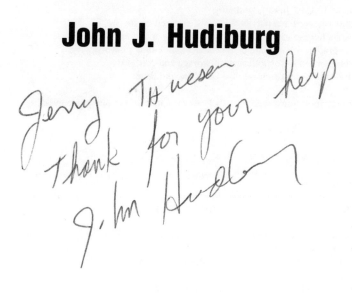

*Jerry Thuesen*
*Thank for your help*
*John Hud...*

**QUALITY RESOURCES**
A Division of The Kraus Organization Limited
White Plains, New York

Most Quality Resources books are available at quantity discounts
when purchased in bulk. For more information contact:

Special Sales Department
Quality Resources
A Division of The Kraus Organization Limited
One Water Street
White Plains, New York 10601

800-247-8519      914-761-9600

Printed in the United States of America

95 94 93 92 91   10 9 8 7 6 5 4 3 2 1

Quality Resources
A Division of The Kraus Organization Limited
One Water Street, White Plains, New York 10601

Library of Congress Cataloging-in-Publication Data
Hudiburg, John J., 1928–
     Winning with quality : the FPL story / John J. Hudiburg.
       p.   cm.
     Includes bibliographical references and index.
     ISBN 0-527-91646-3
     1. Electric utilities—Florida—Quality control.   2. FPL Group
(Firm)   I. Title.
TK24.F6H83   1991
658.5′62—dc20                                                    91-2235
                                                                    CIP

*This book is dedicated
to the fifteen thousand employees
of the Florida Power & Light Company.*

# Contents

# *Preface*

**W**inning *with Quality* describes the experiences of Florida Power & Light (FPL) in establishing a total quality management (TQM) system: how we went about this process, the elements and principles of our TQM system, the mistakes we made, what we learned, and the results we obtained.

It tells the story of how we at FPL learned, one day at a time, to manage for quality using mostly a Japanese quality management system. It gives the "five W's and an H"—the what, why, who, when, where, and how of our journey—so that readers can learn from our experience and improve the quality of their own companies.

Am I betraying any confidences placed in me by our Japanese teachers? Absolutely not. While some Japanese businesspeople may not feel so magnanimous, the Japanese men and women I know and have learned from want to improve the overall level of quality everywhere. Knowing full well that others will apply the knowledge they impart, our Japanese friends think of this as a benefit for themselves as well as for everyone else, rather than as a sort of leak of proprietary information. The Japanese are becoming more global in their thinking, and their willingness and desire to share their expertise is a prime example of that process.

Those Japanese managers and experts who share this vision of the world's future are as public-spirited as anyone, anywhere, without exception, and I admire them as fellow citizens of the global village.

While I have great respect for the Japanese and what they have been able to accomplish, I also want American companies to prosper and grow stronger. If this is to happen, American companies must be able to compete with the best in the world in the quality arena. I very much want to see this as our future, and I believe that FPL's experience can serve as a model for others.

It might be reasonable to ask why I have chosen to say anything on the matter of quality when others far wiser than I have done their very best. We at FPL have learned to apply our lessons: we are practitioners, not theorists. Ours is the experience of doing. We read the books and were just as confused as anyone ever was, but we were determined to apply what we learned. We made our mistakes and then we came back and tried again. Step by step we began to master the process. As we digested one phase, we bit off some more and chewed on that. As Dr. Noriaki Kano, one of our counselors, told us, you don't get to play center field for the New York Yankees by reading a book on baseball. Nor do you get there by watching the Yankees play. To play the game like a champion, you must get down on the field and take part in the real thing. And you must practice and practice and practice, and then you have to play the game against the very best.

For those who would install a total quality management system, it is no longer necessary to go to Japan. In 1984, when FPL decided to implement TQM, I felt we had to do it that way; but now more and more American companies are becoming proficient in their own application of TQM.

I want this book to be a road map for those many other companies who realize that they too must start on their own quality journey—a journey that every company must take if it is to remain successful in the twenty-first century. It is said that a trip of a thousand miles begins with the first step, and it is time for us in America to take many such steps. Reading this book will not teach you everything you need to know in the twenty-first century, but it may be a first step. One story should illustrate just how necessary the journey is.

Recently I was in Istanbul at the home of Mr. Sakip Sabanci, a leading industrialist in Turkey. Among his other activities, he is in the tire-making business. During my visit, I had a chance to talk to my host about one of his recent joint ventures. I knew something about each of the three companies involved in the negotiations and about their views of themselves, and was fascinated to hear the other side of the story.

Mr. Sabanci's company was going to expand its tire-manufacturing capabilities in Turkey and was looking for a strong, non-Turkish partner. They had considered Goodyear, whom they knew well and regarded highly. But they were also talking to Bridgestone, the major Japanese tire manufacturer.

By way of background, in the course of regular visits to companies with good reputations for quality my colleagues at FPL and I had visited both Goodyear and Bridgestone, each of whom thought they made higher-quality tires than the other. In fact, Bob Mercer, the chairman of Goodyear, had been quite adamant about his company's quality improvement progress and high-quality products when I talked to him a year before my trip to Turkey. He had certainly seemed to me personally dedicated to high quality, and he had credibility because he could back up his statements with data.

On the other hand, we had visited Bridgestone somewhat before my last encounter with Mercer at Goodyear. At Bridgestone we had seen a Japanese-style quality improvement system that made a very strong impression on us. Three years ago, if anyone had asked me, I would have said that when it came to quality Goodyear and Bridgestone were about equal but that Bridgestone would make more rapid progress because of its systematic way of going about quality improvement.

Now, in Istanbul, I was about to hear from Mr. Sabanci, the man who had made the decision on whether Goodyear or Bridgestone would be his future partner.

In his opinion, both companies had the potential to be strong partners. In fact, he said that in a number of ways they were almost equal, except for one thing: Bridgestone had a clear lead in its quality program. Not only was it somewhat better at this time, but in his opinion the gap was widening. He felt that for this reason the Japanese were going to be the leading tire manufacturer in the world, and this was the only kind of partner Mr. Sabanci wanted to have. Sad to say, there were no prizes for second place.

Because I had by then seen the power of the Japanese quality system working at FPL, I understood what he was saying. I was equally sure, however, that Bob Mercer would not agree.

Why is it that Americans, or others, so frequently lose out when they are in competition with Japanese companies? More importantly, why do consumers in a free market so often choose products made by Japanese over all others? Are Japanese products really the best value and are consumers making the proper choice, or is their success a result of unfair competition or some particular kind of Far Eastern skillfulness?

It is not my purpose nor is it within my power to defend every Japanese company's activities. But in most cases I strongly believe that consumers *are* making wise choices and know exactly what they are doing. How did this come about? How has Japanese management done such a fantastic job of transforming their companies into international superstars? Why is the quality of their goods and services so high, and improving? Their competition in the United States and elsewhere is getting better, and yet, if anything, the quality gap appears to be widening. I think I know how they do it. The Japanese taught me and my associates how, openly and without any reservations.

Of course, there are no secrets about any management system, at least not for long. Many excellent books have been written on the system of quality management used by leading Japanese companies. Texts written by the leading experts in Japan have been translated into English and can be obtained at any good bookstore. American management experts have written their own books on the subject after visiting Japanese companies and being shown openly what is being done. Yet American managers who read these books and try to use the system don't seem to get it quite right. They may come close, or they may do parts of the program well, but, again, there are no prizes for second place. Why don't we do as well? Where is the breakdown occurring?

My FPL colleagues and I have paid the price over four long, hard years to learn some of the answers to these questions. It is this learning experience that I hope to convey through this book.

# Getting Started

*I*t was Friday evening, the 18th of August 1989. The occasion was the celebration after the conclusion of our Deming Prize audit. We had just finished two weeks of an intensive examination by eight Japanese university professors who had thoroughly reviewed our quality improvement activities from top to bottom. Not just top management, but middle managers, first-line supervisors, and also journeymen, meter readers, clerks, and others, had stood up and told their quality stories.

And they had quite a story to tell. They had brought about dramatic improvements, knew exactly how they had done it, and were proud of their accomplishments. Now they were ready to celebrate. It was one of those rare instances in a lifetime, when a group does something important as a team. They had been working arduously for four years to perfect a companywide quality improvement process. They had been practicing for the Deming exam every weekend for the last four months. Now, they had just nailed it, and they knew it.

There was a glow on every face. The band started playing a Latin beat, shifted to rock and roll, to country, and threw in a golden oldie or two for people like me; then they did it all over

1

again except maybe a little louder. As I looked on, I remembered the scenes of the celebration in Times Square on VJ Day.

Several people came up to me and suggested that I write a book about our experiences. Sure, I thought, but first build a statue of a fool and name it John!

The following month, I made a speech in Europe on the subject of quality management. The speech seemed to go over very well, and my ego was really pumped up.

When I got to the airport for my return home, however, my ego was quickly deflated as I returned to the more familiar real world. The area around the ticket counter was like a mob scene from some old World War II movie—total confusion. Masses of displaced persons of all ages, each with his or her own pile of bundles and baggage, were packed in wall-to-wall. By the time my wife and I finally got through this mess and onto the plane, we were an hour late. Then we had to wait at least another hour for the last of the passengers to straggle on board. Everyone, passengers and crew alike, was in a bad mood by the time we took off. From then on things just got worse. You might say we were flying in the losers bracket. We missed our connection in Frankfurt and had to start improvising as we went along. By the time we got to Heathrow in London, we were eight hours late. Then we were twelve hours late into Kennedy. In fact, our plane was the last one in from Europe that night. (It was the one with mechanical problems.) While we were waiting for one last plane to return us to Miami, I began to think about what we had done at Florida Power & Light and about the enormous improvements we had been able to achieve in customer service and satisfaction. I reflected on this, and compared it to the string of air travel experiences I had just gone through.

All day long, time after time, I had seen a world crying out for a better management system. I don't think managers and employees want to do a poor job. They don't enjoy working all day with angry, dissatisfied customers. And yet, everywhere one goes the need for improved quality is manifest. Everyone knows that there has to be a better way. People don't want someone giving them hell all day long. What they want is help—a way to make things better. I decided that I should write that book about FPL after all.

---

### FLORIDA POWER & LIGHT

Florida Power & Light (FPL) is the fourth largest and fastest growing electric utility in the U.S. Currently the primary investor-owned subsidiary of FPL Group, Inc., a diversified holding company organized in 1984, the utility was established in 1925 to supply reliable electric light and power to parts of southeastern Florida.

The present-day service area, broken into five major divisions (Northeastern, Eastern, Southeastern, Southern, and Western), encompasses the east coast of Florida and virtually the whole lower half of the state (27,650 sq. mi.), providing power to 6 million residents (3 million customer accounts). With its General Office (GO) in Miami, the company operates thirteen power plants (total capacity 16,000 megawatts), two of them nuclear (St. Lucie and Turkey Point). It also runs 45 customer service offices, 72 service centers, and pays nearly 15,000 employees from an operating budget of $4.75 billion.

FPL's retail electricity rates are regulated by the Florida Public Service Commission (FPSC), while its wholesale rates are regulated by the Federal Energy Regulatory Commission (FERC). Nuclear power plant operations are regulated by the Nuclear Regulatory Commission (NRC), and environmental regulations are overseen by various federal, state, and local agencies.

---

The Florida Power & Light Company is an electric utility company that serves about half the state of Florida, mainly on the east coast. Its 15,000 employees have been working very hard to improve the satisfaction of its three million customers and they have been very successful. They have reduced customer complaints by 70 percent, and company surveys show that the percentage of customers extremely satisfied has increased from 41 percent to 62 percent—an all-time high. In fact, they have been able to achieve equally dramatic improvement in one thing after another: service availability, reliability, nuclear plant safety, employee safety, and employee satisfaction, to mention a few. As a result of these improvements, FPL was able to reduce the price of electricity to its customers, reversing an inflationary trend. I know that what FPL has been able to accomplish can be repeated in any other organization. Our management system works, and works to produce quality goods and services in a manner that is far more effective than any other system of which I am aware.

Our quest for a new management system began in 1984 when FPL became dissatisfied with its existing quality improvement program. At that time we had a very active quality improvement team program, but we felt we needed more. The team program alone would not be enough to help us achieve our newly conceived vision of becoming the best-managed electric utility in the United States. FPL was facing a number of internal and external pressures. The company's rapid growth between the 1940s and the 1970s had encouraged the development of an unwieldy management structure, and we found ourselves unable to respond quickly enough to a rapidly changing business climate. We needed a management system that would allow us to cope with these problems—and that would enable us to plan for future changes.

Accordingly, we began to look around for a complete quality management *system,* something much more comprehensive than just teams. We looked throughout the United States at many fine companies who had good reputations and were doing an excellent job. We investigated various management programs that were generally available in the marketplace and that were well regarded: things like management by objectives and zero-based budgets. In fact, we had used these and other techniques as well.

They were all good in their own way, but none was the comprehensive system we wanted, and none was adequately geared to helping us address the pressing issue of customer satisfaction. So we continued to search. Late in 1984, a group of our management personnel including myself went to Japan to observe the companywide total quality management system practiced there. We looked at a number of different companies, which fortunately included Kansai Electric Power Company in Osaka. Because Kansai and FPL are in the same business, use the same equipment, and have many of the same problems, we were able to relate very well to Kansai's situation. Their application of the quality management system was particularly relevant to FPL, and their results were impressive.

We paid a second visit to Kansai Power Company in the summer of 1985, and spent two full weeks looking into what they were doing and the results they had achieved. It was after this visit that we elected to go lock, stock, and barrel with the Japanese style of quality management. Before this second trip I had been more than a little cool toward companywide quality improvement programs. But the results Kansai was getting were so impressive, I became convinced that FPL should become a total quality company. In September 1985, I announced to the company that we would proceed with a full implementation of our Quality Improvement Program (QIP). At that point, we knew we didn't fully understand what they were doing, but we were determined to learn everything about it.

With the help of Kansai Electric, we were most fortunate to obtain a number of excellent Japanese counselors, who agreed to teach us the system and assist us in implementing it at FPL. These

# THE DEMING PRIZE

Named after W. Edwards Deming, the famous American statistician and founding figure in modern quality control, the Deming Prize was instituted in Japan in 1951 in order to spur productive activities and promote the use of statistical methods as a management tool. The prize is awarded annually (in November) in two main categories:

- The Deming Application Prize, awarded to companies, divisions, and small enterprises in recognition of outstanding success in the practice of quality control.
- The Deming Prize for Individuals, awarded to persons in recognition of outstanding contributions in the area of research and education.

The prize is generally considered the most prestigious honor of its kind in Japan. It was officially opened to overseas companies in 1986.

The prize is overseen and administered by the Union of Japanese Scientists and Engineers (JUSE), an independent, nonprofit body of quality control experts from universities and research institutions. JUSE works to advance quality practices in industry, and its Deming Prize Committee evaluates corporate award applicants in such areas as quality policies and objectives, organization and management, employee education and dissemination of quality control concepts, product and process quality, analysis of information, standardization and utilization of statistical methods, and planning for continued quality improvement. A key objective behind the prize process is to stimulate people and companies to go beyond mere conformance to standards and lead them to discover ways to adapt total quality management to their own organization.

The examination process starts with an initial application and eligibility test, followed by a detailed written description of company quality practices. After that, an extensive site examination is performed by Prize Committee members. There is no fee for filing an application, but expenses incurred in connection with the site examination (including transportation and translators) must be met by the applicant.

The Deming Application Prize can be awarded to more than one company (it is essentially noncompetitive) or it may not be issued at all in a given year. If a company fails to satisfy the award criteria, it is assigned a "pending" status until it feels prepared to complete the exam. Previous awardees include Hitachi, Mitsubishi, Fuji Photo, Nippon Steel, Nissan, Toyota, and Matsushita.

counselors were affiliated with the Union of Japanese Scientists and Engineers (JUSE), a nonprofit organization established to promote advanced science and technology in industry. JUSE is also the organization that administrates and directs the Deming Prize. We were especially fortunate to have Dr. Tetsuichi Asaka agree to be our lead counselor. Dr. Asaka is one of the small group that has led the quality movement from the very beginning. What was more important from our point of view was that he is the foremost educator of the TQM process in Japan.

Our desire from the start was to become practitioners of the same system we had seen, and we asked our Japanese counselors to teach us just as they would any of their Japanese clients. Our progress and our speed of assimilation were about the same as a Japanese company would have expected, and our results are also comparable to those of Japanese companies. In every manner, what we have accomplished at FPL is typical of what a Japanese company following the same path would accomplish. The rather profound difference is that FPL is an American company located in Florida. To the best of my knowledge, at this time we are the only company in the United States that has established a Japanese-style total quality management system. Many companies have implemented part of the system, and the subsidiaries of American companies in Japan have adopted the total system, but in 1985, when FPL elected to go companywide with the Japanese system, we were pioneers.

During the Deming Prize examination, I was asked, "What was the unique thing that FPL contributed to the advancement of the quality process?" I responded that we had gone to Japan, taken the management system so widely used by their best companies, studied it, and learned how to use it. We then installed it within an American electric utility company, with its wide diversity of employees and customers, which is so typical of what you would expect to see throughout the United States. This was our unique contribution. It was a mark of our achievement that before this, any examiner for the Deming Prize would have been conducting the exam in Japan speaking Japanese, whereas for this exam, the examiners were in Miami speaking to us through an interpreter. This was definitely a first.

FPL is the first company outside Japan ever to be awarded the Deming Application Prize. We used the application process itself as a means of putting pressure on ourselves to learn to apply the quality system thoroughly and rapidly.

We believe we have proven that this management system can be transported to the United States, and that it will work in an American electric utility company the same way it works in Japan. In a broader sense, I feel we have also proven that the total quality management system will work in any kind of company anywhere in the world. The four principles on which it is based, customer satisfaction, the use of data and analysis, the plan-do-check-act cycle (also known as the Deming cycle) of continuous improvement, and respect for people, are universally applicable. They are not the product of some special element within Asian culture. They are the product of many years of thought and effort by many people who have a clear insight into human nature. These four principles, if properly applied, will be equally successful anywhere in the world.

To all who are dedicated to providing quality services and products to customers and who sense the necessity of using a more comprehensive system to obtain better results, my advice is to get started—and I wish you good luck.

In the highly competitive worldwide markets that will emerge in the twenty-first century, only those companies able to do an excellent job in providing quality and customer satisfaction are going to survive and prosper. As we move toward a truly worldwide market, with companies from the new European Common Market, the Pacific Rim, North America, and the newly freed Eastern European countries all in vigorous competition, and as goods and services from all areas of the world become readily available and consumers are well informed about quality, prices, and other product characteristics, competition will be like nothing we have ever seen before. I am convinced that American companies can compete and can be successful through quality management. Many American companies are doing an excellent job now. Others can learn to apply the quality management process, and prosper. To survive when you're up against world-class competition you must yourself be world class, and many U.S. companies are not going to measure up.

American management must be free to take a longer-term perspective and concentrate on satisfying the customer, and by doing so gain market share, sustain corporate health, and continue to earn good profits. But to do this, their focus must be on quality and on the needs and desires of the consumer rather than just on the next quarter's earnings, possibilities of hostile takeovers, and other short-term matters. American management must be allowed and encouraged to make and carry out successful long-term strategies. The very strong companies against which we will compete have a long-range view of their future direction, they are dedicated to their customers, and they have a strategy for how to achieve their vision. To succeed, American management must find a way to do the same thing. The road we in the United States have been following will lead many a well-known American corporation to ruin. We need to examine and eliminate those governmental regulations and tax laws that reward speculation and short-term gains and create instead a business environment that rewards long-term strategies and goals.

One way or another, companies in the United States must

provide quality goods and services or as a nation we will sink into second-class status. But even if our government policies were perfect, if we produce junk that no one wants to buy, we are still in trouble. Installing a Japanese-style total quality management system, as FPL has done, is part of the answer, and we believe that our experience can help others get started by serving as a model of the quality process.

As I review FPL's experience in this book, I will describe the five components of the management system—policy management, quality improvement teams, quality in daily work, vendor quality, and bright ideas—followed by a look at such supporting activities as education, training, and recognition. I will look at some of the mistakes we made and what we were able to learn from them. Finally, I will discuss the massive effort we put into the Deming Prize challenge, covering not only what we did and how, but also why we did it. It was an immense amount of work but it was worth it. One of our officers likened it to plebe year at the Naval Academy—something he wouldn't have missed for anything, but something he never wanted to do again.

We used to assure our employees that when our quality improvement program was fully installed, working at FPL would be fun. During the time we were preparing for the Deming exam, I saw some posters on the walls asking, "Is this the fun?" Our people certainly didn't lose their sense of humor during the hard times, and I can assure you, our celebration party after the exam *was* a lot of fun. More important, the people at FPL have experienced that soul-satisfying pleasure that comes from doing an important job very well indeed.

# The Vision

$Y$ou must start somewhere, for in the beginning there is chaos. Well, perhaps the situation isn't that bad, but total quality management (TQM) needs a beginning, and this means determining right up front what the CEO's vision is for the company. A vision is a dramatic picture of the future that has the power to motivate and inspire. This vital first step is where many companies go astray. Of the entire TQM implementation process, this step requires the most fundamental thinking by top management. What business are you in? What products or services do you supply now? In the future? What human needs do you and your company fulfill? What is the prime purpose of the company: to make money or to serve the needs of mankind? Who are your customers? What do your customers desire? What is management's role and how do you go about carrying it out? What is the most important thing you do? How do you measure your progress? What are your goals? What are your strategies?

Many managements feel they have a solid grasp of the answers to these questions. But when they are asked to state them out loud or in writing, they realize that there are large gaps in their ability to articulate them clearly and understandably. Moreover, if one compares the answers to these questions as given by all the officers of a company, there are usually interesting differences. At least there were in our case. I don't think we had a very clear understanding of the answers to these questions in the beginning. In any event, if top management can't state them consistently and clearly, how can anyone else in the organization know what they have in mind?

At first, some of our officers would have said that the purpose of any company is to make money. I do not believe this. Making money is a necessary by-product of a more basic purpose. Others, including myself, would have said that the purpose of FPL is to supply safe, reliable, reasonably priced electric service to our customers. While this comes closer to what FPL is all about, it is a mission statement, not a vision. It does not have the power to inspire anyone, nor does it show any intent to be a leader.

It was 1984 when we decided to develop our new corporate vision. But at that time we already had a running start in the process. In fact, our first steps toward quality improvement had begun in 1981.

The chairman and chief executive officer at that time, Marshall McDonald, had an open mind and a ready willingness to try new ideas. In 1981, management held some discussions about quality improvement and what it could do for us. We had had some contact with formal quality control in the nuclear power area. We were in the process of building our fourth nuclear power plant, and within the nuclear organization we had departments with names like "quality control" and "quality assurance." While the activities of these departments in those days had little or no relationship to the Japanese quality management system we later installed, they did get us thinking about the subject of quality improvement. Some of our people read the books of the day on quality and generally knew what was happening in the quality improvement area. We had organized our construction activities in a manner that we felt would produce quality assurance and control. And we did have some success even in these early days. For example, in 1984 we had completed the construction of the St. Lucie nuclear power plant in only sixty-six months, something of a U.S. record at the time. In retrospect, it is clear that whatever success we had was due more to the hard work and skill of the individuals involved than to any quality management system. However, we did have the feel of success and we wanted to do more. As a result of our discussions in 1981, the decision was made to implement quality improvement teams in the nonnuclear parts of the company.

By the end of 1982, we had formed seventy quality improvement teams. The installation and workings of these teams is covered in Chapter 6. Subsequently, each new step we took led to small successes, and at the time we needed all the success we could get.

We had gone through a very difficult period in the 1970s. Two oil shocks, high inflation, falling stock prices, and rising bond interest rates all contributed to an increasingly hostile financial environment. Meanwhile, increasing governmental regulation of nuclear power, as a result of the Three Mile Island accident in 1979, and increasing environmental regulation added to the external pressures FPL was facing. The price of electricity was rising faster than the Consumer Price Index, and our customers were becoming less and less satisfied with the level of service they were receiving. All of this had left both us and our customers in a sad state.

I am often asked why an electric utility that is a monopoly would be so dedicated to achieving quality. My answer is, first, that the quality management system is the most effective way I know to cope with problems. Second, in the uncertain environment of the future, if we are in solid with our customers, we will be in better shape to survive. Finally, the management and employees of FPL take pride in what they do and want to do even better, and our quality management system lets them do that. In short, we use quality management for the same reasons that any other company would. But in the early 1980s we didn't have this system, and we were in trouble. We were not coping very well with problems, our customers were angry at us, and employees didn't take much pride in the fact that they worked for FPL.

But by 1984 things seemed to stabilize somewhat. The price of the fuel we used to make electricity even went down a little. With a calmer environment in which to do business and with some success with quality teams, we found ourselves with a little breathing room.

This is where we were when we began to take a very deep look at ourselves. We wanted to figure out just who we were and what we wanted to be—in short, what our vision should be—and to try to develop some long-range plans for our future progress. To help us with this investigation, we brought in the McKinsey Company as consultants to diagnose what our strong points were, what our weaknesses were, and to tell us what they thought might be the points on which we could build. They told us that we were a very well managed electric utility—not the best, but well managed—and that we certainly had the potential to become one of the best. They urged us to drop our old mission statement and to develop a totally new corporate vision.

The other officers of the company and I had a number of stimulating meetings to discuss this and other issues, some of them running well into the evening—wide-ranging discussions of our circumstance, our position within our own industry, within society generally, with our customers, and so on. In the process we discarded our earlier views about who we were and what we wanted to become and at the end of all this, we developed our new corporate vision which stated, "During the next decade, we want to become the best-managed electric utility in the United States and an excellent company overall and be recognized as such." We thought through literally every word in that vision, which was designed to be primarily for internal communication to our employees to let them know what management thought the company was all about. But of course we recognized that it would be communicated outside the company as well, and we were concerned that it convey to both groups a realistic but ambitious view of where we thought we should be headed.

"During the next decade" was the easiest part. We wanted to state a distinct period of time so that the vision was more than just an open-ended dream that would drift into the future and never be realized. An objective without a date is a hope; an objective with a date is a goal. We chose "the next decade" because we felt this was a realistic period of time given our uncertainty about how we were going to accomplish the task.

In the statement "to become the best-managed electric utility," the first consideration was "electric utility." We decided that FPL would be solely an electric utility company. At this time, we had been considering the issue of diversification, but we decided that any such expansions would have to be achieved through creating new and separate companies. We felt that each pot should stand on its own bottom, and decided that FPL itself would be a pure vanilla electric utility and nothing else.

Next we considered the words "best-managed." "Best" is a key word. It implies a very precise thing to most people. It is not the same as a "good" electric utility, or a "better" electric utility. We could have picked other words but we chose, "the best," meaning number one. At one point we talked about whether the word "best" would be taken as arrogance by people in other utilities. But we reasoned that if some other utility wanted to challenge us on this, so much the better; we would both stand to win.

But best what? Best-*managed.* Why managed? We argued over this word for a long, long time. How would we know we were the best? Well, for example, our company team could win the championship softball tournament. But that isn't what we mean by best. We could have the highest earnings or the lowest rates or the best safety record, etc. But we knew that we couldn't do all of these things at the same time because in some cases they are mutually exclusive. "Best-managed" implied that our goal should be the coordination and optimization of conflicting objectives. That is, our overall result should be the best; we didn't have to be the best in every way as measured against every other utility at all times. In short, we needed an optimized overall result. So we chose to be the "best-managed." This did cause a problem in that most employees, especially at that time, didn't consider themselves to be managers. It took several years to make it clear to all of our employees that, more and more, they would be expected to manage their own jobs. This was reinforced through team activities, which involved all levels of employees in many tasks that were traditionally considered management functions.

The next part of our vision statement, "an excellent company overall," extended this same point. In other words, every company activity should be involved and should be excellent. Achieving this would require the best from each employee. But something more was meant by "an excellent company overall." We wanted to be considered as an excellent company at the national level—not just within the narrow framework of the electric utility industry, but as an excellent company overall compared to all others.

And then there is the phrase, "and be recognized as such." Again, we didn't think it would be enough if we just went around saying, "We're the greatest." We thought that recognition would be far more meaningful if it came from others. Above all, we wanted our customers to recognize us as the best-managed electric utility and an excellent company overall. So, in time, we developed benchmarking criteria with which to measure our own progress in relation to that of fifteen other electric utilities. We chose areas for comparison that were important from the point of view of our customers and for which good data existed.

Thus was each and every word of our vision carefully considered, not only in terms of its meaning to us, but also in terms of how other people might interpret it. We especially tried to see how it would be seen and interpreted by our employees, our stockholders, and our customers. With our establishment of the new FPL vision in 1984, we concluded this early phase of our quest for total quality.

We were rather proud of the results of our efforts. Immediately thereafter we announced the new corporate vision to the rest of the company. We thought of this vision as being chiseled in stone over the portals of FPL. And while we knew that we had some work to do before we would be "the best," we rested for a while after our creative efforts were over.

Twice a year we held what we called Situation Conferences at FPL. These were two-day meetings between top and middle management to exchange information on the company's situation. At the first meeting after we had formulated our vision, someone asked if we were serious about becoming the best-managed electric utility. The reply was, "Of course we mean it!" The next question was "How?" As I recall, the answer was something to the effect that the matter would require further study.

At various industry meetings in the early 1980s, FPL's chairman, Marshall McDonald, had become acquainted with some of the officers of both Tokyo Electric and Kansai Electric in Japan, and since then, there had been several visits back and forth between some employees of our companies. We were especially interested in Kansai Electric because they were installing a quality management system.

Then in November of 1984, our friends at Kansai Electric Power Company in Osaka, under the leadership of their president, Mr. Shoichiro Kobayashi, won the Deming Application Prize for Quality. We were impressed and we wanted to congratulate them. Also, we were curious to see what they had done to win the prize. In late November of that year some of the officers, including our executive vice president Bob Tallon and myself, went to Japan, as I mentioned earlier. We had arranged to visit other Deming Prize-winning companies on the way to Osaka. When these companies described how they managed for quality, we tried to look intelligent, but in truth we didn't understand a tenth of what they were talking about. They were truly speaking a foreign language. Finally, when we got to Osaka and Kansai Electric Company, things were a little better. We had a better understanding of their business and they were very patient in explaining their activities to us. Their progress in quality improvement was an amazing eye opener. In some ways we had been better than they were in 1981, but they had made steady and substantial progress and had passed us by, and in most cases left us far behind. We still didn't understand how they had done it, but we really understood the results. We were fascinated with their process and efforts. We were also very glad that we did not have to compete with Kansai. (Even their softball team was better than ours: a year later, during another visit, their team beat ours 28 to 2.)

In an effort to understand their system better, we sent more of our employees to visit Kansai. And then some of the officers and I returned the next summer and spent considerable time studying Kansai's process. After we returned home, we held several discussions about what we had seen at Kansai. Our conclusion was that with some help, we could and *should* put in our own version of a TQM system. We asked Kansai to assist us with our efforts, and they agreed to help. Without the assistance of Kansai I do not know whether we could even have attempted this implementation.

Early on, we learned that there are four principles upon which the entire process is based: customer satisfaction, management by fact, the plan-do-check-act (PDCA) cycle, and respect for people. I will discuss each of these further, but the first and foremost is customer satisfaction. The Japanese study the customer. Then they study the customer again. Their entire process, internal as well as external, is directed toward the customer. By serving the customer they believe they will gain market share and corporate health. It is taken as a given that if they are better than anyone else at serving the customer, they will have strong sales and thereby make greater profits. Their ideology says first comes customer satisfaction, then sales, then profits. I think this ideology is one reason why they have been so successful at total quality management (TQM). This was the customer-driven quality management system we needed and had been searching for.

After considerable discussion, we adopted the following definition for quality: Quality is meeting our customers' needs, expectations, and desires. In other words, customer satisfaction and quality are so closely linked as to be the same. Two very important concepts are included in this definition of quality. First, we were not talking about "little q" quality, or adherence to standards, but we meant rather a broader concept that we call "big Q" quality, encompassing safety, quality, price, delivery, etc. Second, the purpose of all the quality improvement effort would be focused on what we did for the customer. Our employees enthusiastically embraced this idea and worked very hard to support it. I do not believe, on the other hand, that American employees will work nearly as hard if they are given only the narrow objective of increasing profits or improving productivity.

The fundamental assumption is that if you do good things for your customers, then it follows good things will happen for your stockholders and employees. Conversely, if you do not do good things for customers, you have no sales, no earnings, and no employees.

It becomes very clear that since the organization is made up of people and operates in a social environment, it must do a good job in filling some human need. No organization that relies on customers should ever get confused on this very basic and fundamental point.

I am sure you are saying to yourself, "Of course, I know that." But just look around you and see how often you can observe management making short-term decisions that increase current profits at the expense of long-term customer good will. The idea of taking a long-term approach to corporate well-being may have come more easily to us because FPL is an electric utility. It is characteristic of utilities to make long-term investments and to have rather stable revenues and profits. Of course, all companies must have profits to survive and grow. However, major American companies who have been and intend to be in business for many years, and who otherwise have strong profits, still fall into the trap of the quick fix. Then in the following year they feel they have to try to top themselves. They can easily get themselves into a death spiral of one short-term expediency after another. In no way are these companies going to be able to compete with firms whose principal focus is customer satisfaction over the long term. In some cases American management has been forced by circumstances to take short-term expediency steps, but all too many others who have followed this road really did not have to. It's tragic.

So, the first major lesson we learned from the Japanese is that quality is meeting customers' needs, wants, and desires over the long haul. This is the foundation upon which any effective quality program must rest.

While I was answering questions for the third time during the Deming exam, with about one hour left in the final week, I was asked, "Mr. Hudiburg, based on your experience in installing a Japanese-style management system at FPL, what three pieces of advice would you give another American CEO who was considering doing the same thing?" I thought then, and still do, that this is a very good question.

My response had three main points. First, I would strongly advise other CEOs to follow our experience because the results stood to be nothing short of spectacular, and I only knew of this one way that they could be achieved. I would tell them that they could attain levels of quality and customer satisfaction greater than they had ever imagined. Moreover, they would enjoy work more than ever before in their life. But they should proceed only if they and their top management were absolutely convinced that this was what they should do. They would encounter hurdles and disappointments, and have doubts along the way. Therefore, they should be convinced that it was the right thing to do before they started.

Second, they should be prepared to make a commitment to their employees in education and training beyond anything they had ever done before. Both they and all their employees would need to learn both the theory and practice of the system. We gave all of our employees both formal and on-the-job-training, and ultimately developed thirteen in-house employee training programs on quality. Employees need to study and make their inevitable mistakes, then learn more, correct the mistakes, and learn more, over and over. In short, practice, practice, and more practice.

Finally, I said that anyone interested in quality management must consider it as a *complete management system.* It is not something to be delegated to a quality department, nor is it something to be done in addition to regular work. It *is* the regular work. It is the way that all employees manage their work. Quality improvement teams and, indeed, all of the other parts of the TQM system are each well worth doing in their own rights, and each produces very positive benefits. But it is all of them working together in a systematic way that produces the dramatic results companies really want. And while a company would probably want to introduce each component of the TQM system separately, it should plan from the very beginning to implement all the components.

It must have been a satisfactory answer—we won the Deming Prize. Moreover, I believe that this answer is the same one I would give today. Of course, the Deming Prize challenge was only the means to install total quality management at FPL—not an end in itself—just as TQM was the means to improve customer satisfaction. To put it another way, all of this effort was our way of setting about achieving our vision to be the best-managed electric utility company.

# Top Management
# Commitment

$S$ince I left the active work force of Florida Power & Light in January 1990, I have been traveling to various companies to talk to their management about how they might initiate a quality improvement process or program. I have been fascinated by the questions I am asked and the various stages of development I observe. It is like *déjà vu.* I can see FPL at the different stages in our own journey. I am often asked the same question I fielded during the Deming exam: What advice would I give to the management of a company thinking about putting in a total quality program? I try my very best to make the point that top management has to be convinced that it's the right thing for them to do and has to play a personal role in leading the journey. A few examples should illustrate some of the more common levels of top management understanding and commitment present in different companies.

In the first stage of development, a company's management is typically working very hard, using a traditional management style, and doing about the best they can following this approach. They have developed their own corporate culture, which has served them fairly well. Generally, in America, this first stage also includes a top-down hierarchical management style. The situation is what one would see in many, many companies: each manager has been successfully following an individual approach developed over a lifetime of experience, and whatever they have learned by this time is pretty deeply ingrained in their thinking. However, by reading various magazines and attending seminars, managers have become aware that there is something of interest going on in the quality improvement area.

Now this company, like any other, would contend that it produces products of good quality. Indeed, in talking to management throughout the world, I have yet to meet a single manager who doesn't believe that his or her company, or department, produces quality. (I understand that a Mr. Shoddy was a textile manufacturer who supplied material to the Union Army during the Civil War. I suppose that even he, if asked, would have asserted that his shoddy cloth was of good quality.)

But this first-stage management team is listening and reading. They recognize that whatever they have done in the past is probably not going to be good enough in the future, and that there is some sort of system that various companies are using to improve quality. So they begin to make inquiries into where they might find out more about such a system. They have at least accepted the idea that they probably will need to change.

Today, there is an enormous interest in quality improvement in America, and many companies are at this first stage. The National Institute of Standards and Technology mailed 180,000 copies of the Malcolm Baldrige National Quality Award information package in 1990, in response to requests they had received. Florida Power & Light currently receives about seventy calls a week from various organizations that have heard about it. These organizations ask if they can visit FPL or have someone from FPL visit them and explain our experience to them. They want to understand better what we did, how we did it, and how they might implement something similar. Many of these calls come from companies that are already deeply involved in quality improvement, but many come from companies that are just getting started.

Typically the managers of these companies are quite skeptical and are afraid that it will mean additional work or force a change in their long-cherished beliefs. They are generally concerned about just what it will mean for them personally, as well as for their organizations. And believe me, they are quite chary about making a big commitment to quality improvement. I try to encourage them in every way I can. I remember that this was how I felt in the beginning. I had no understanding of just what TQM was or of the tremendous results that can be obtained with it. It is hard to be fired up about something when you don't understand it. Likewise, in the early stages, many of FPL's officers told me of their concerns and objections to such a major shift in the way we did things. We talked about how much it would cost or how much disruption it would cause the organization. The unstated, but nonetheless real fear was that we would have to change our familiar way of thinking and acting. I wish I were gifted enough to inspire every other company's management to get started in earnest. Unfortunately, I have not been entirely successful in that regard. To illustrate this point, I will describe a few real-life examples.

The first example is a company in a service industry. There are numerous competitors in the industry, but it is essentially dominated by this company and two others. The company has a few large customers who are demanding improved services, greater diversity, greater flexibility, and shorter lead times. This particular company believes itself to be the technological leader in its industry and thinks it is doing a good job in quality now. At this point, their approach to meeting increased demands has been to mechanize their processes using robotics and computers. They are very proud of their leadership in the industry and want to maintain their position.

Some of the company officers are aware that there are quality management systems that could produce improved results, and they have been urging top management to consider implementing such systems. Top management, however, is very skeptical and is reluctant to change; they aren't convinced that a different management system could produce significantly better results, and they are concerned about costs. They don't understand the dramatic improvement that can be made with a rather modest investment in management science technology as opposed to hardware.

In most cases the issue of cost is a straw man. The direct costs involved in TQM are devoted to education and training, and are usually very small when compared to the overall operating expenses of a company. (At FPL these costs were never as much as 1 percent of the overall operation and maintenance budget.) The real issue is fear of change. Top management and about two-thirds of the officers are quite concerned that changing their management system will mean many difficulties and more work. After all, by this time in their careers they have seen a lot of new management fads come and go, and they think this may be just one more. I am told, and I believe, that the companies that have been the most successful have the hardest time embracing total quality management. So this service company's management will continue "looking" until they feel the need to change.

The second example is a large bank in the United States. One of its four major divisions volunteered to be the model within the overall organization to start the quality process. The president of that division of the bank is convinced that he needs to do something (and I am equally convinced that he will do so).

He is aware that some of his competitors are doing a better job in quality and customer service and he is determined that his company do something to catch up. Although he doesn't know very much about what's available, he has been looking into the matter, trying to come up with the best approach for his organization to use, and is eager to get started. He and the officers reporting to him are concerned about what the changes will mean, but at this point top management has completed its investigations and is prepared to start. The entire organization will be involved because very strong direction will be provided from the top. However, they have yet to begin in a systematic, managed way to improve quality.

This bank is typical of more and more American companies today who have gone through the initial examination and analysis phase and have concluded that they need to do *something*. They are poised, as it were, at the threshold. The increasing number of companies at this stage is encouraging—Dr. Joseph Juran, a well-known American quality expert, now says that for the first time he is optimistic about America's prospects in quality.

The bank's approach to quality improvement is top-down in its beginning; the service company's is bottom-up. They are both typical of many companies just getting started. In 1983, FPL had some of both characteristics. At that time I personally doubted that what we were doing with quality improvement teams could produce very dramatic results. We were asking every question we could think of and trying to understand what more could be done, but with a very negative frame of mind, totally unsold. If a few of us had not changed our thinking, we most likely would not have gone any further. So I can see myself especially in the first example. I would say also that in many ways the bank is in about the same position we were in after our first trip to Japan in 1984: we had seen enough to convince us to do something more in quality improvement, but we had not yet decided just what that should be.

Another stage in the development is illustrated by the cases of two other companies. The first is a division of a company in the electronics business. Following the top-down path, top management in the parent company has been sending strong messages for about three years that all elements of that company will have a very active and intensive quality improvement program. However, there is lack of top management follow-through. They have left implementation up to the various divisions, and they make only rather cursory examinations to find out what is happening. In this particular division they have all of the slogans and mottos hanging on the wall. They have their written goals and objectives: if you go through the various departments of this division and ask to see their quality improvement program, they can pull down a book and show you where they are now and where they are going to be in three years and in five years. But they are still not meeting their short-term goals, although they can explain to their own satisfaction why this is so. They have implemented some team activity, and they can describe the process and the results of those teams. Some departments within the organization are going at it with the proper spirit, but most are doing just enough to be able to show they are on board.

Essentially, the organization is merely going through the motions. They are getting a few positive results because in any organization there are going to be some energetic people who will get results regardless of the circumstances. But until the division president is convinced that something more should be done, and takes the time to understand what that something more is, quality improvement does not have a very high priority. The program is just drifting with the tide and will continue to drift until the president of this division makes something happen. This isn't likely to occur until the top management of the parent company recognizes that if they mean what they have been saying, they personally must assume the responsibility. And until they begin to make in-depth reviews of the various division programs and to insist on more than token compliance, progress is going to be very slow. I can think of at least four different companies I have seen recently that would fit this general description.

The second example is a large manufacturing company with about fifteen competitors worldwide and with many lines of products, each organized into its own division. The company is at a second stage of bottom-up push with four of its nine divisions very active in quality improvement. They define quality as meeting the customers' needs, are organized to meet those needs, and have gone through a lengthy installation of quality improvement teams. These four divisions have made a very strong beginning, but in the other half of the company almost nothing is taking place. Top management acts as a cheerleader for those departments or divisions that are doing well and gives out a lot of "attaboys." Although they are very proud of what these divisions have done, they are not leading. They are only following along with those under them, who have been the real leaders, instead of insisting that all divisions follow the models already established within the company. They are losing a golden opportunity because they have these successful role models existing within their company right now. Top management needs to get excited and find out the benefits of a total quality system. The entire organization should be directed toward significant long-term goals, and all of the various divisions of the company should install a quality management system.

Those divisions that have chosen to do this are going to do an excellent job; they are going to get considerable results. But how much more they can do will remain limited until top management decides it is really necessary to have a comprehensive, corporatewide, management-directed quality improvement process. Until this happens, they are not going to go much further than they have already.

Again, I see FPL here. We certainly went through this stage. In 1984, when we first began to look at what other companies were doing, we had a very active team program, about 500 active teams that were producing good results. But it wasn't until we took those trips to Japan that we realized just what was available and what startling and dramatic improvements could be made if top management really got involved. Then, and only then, did we install a complete quality improvement management system. In the first half of 1985, we were approximately where this company is today. Certain divisions were doing well. The very top of the company, the chairman, was enthusiastic and acting as a cheerleader, but none of the top management, including the chairman, really understood the entire system. In other words, we had made a lot of progress but were just beginning to realize what lay ahead and to see what could be done if we changed the way we led the company.

An even higher stage of development is represented by companies like those who have won the Malcolm Baldrige National Quality Award, excellent companies such as Xerox, Milliken, Federal Express, IBM, and Cadillac (GM). These companies have had strong top-down leadership directed intensively toward implementing comprehensive quality improvement throughout their organizations. Teams have been in place for a number of years; they are well directed and are supported throughout the organization, with recognition and with systems set up to implement their improvement ideas. The teams are functioning very effectively and efficiently. These companies have looked at their customers and their customers' needs, have established significant long-term goals, and have made progress toward them. They have corporate visions; they have long-term plans; they have short-term plans; they have a well-coordinated overall program. Their corporate cultures support and encourage all of their employees to improve and do their best. These companies have had a lot of success. They've had strong top management quality improvement leadership for a number of years. In some aspects of quality management, they are as good as or better than FPL.

I feel, however, that they are about at the stage where FPL was in 1988 with regard to policy management. It was at this stage that top management focused the entire company toward breakthrough improvements in customer satisfaction. This is the legacy of our Japanese approach to total quality, and I will cover this more fully in Chapter 5 and in the chapters describing our challenge for the Deming Application Prize. The progress of FPL from the time we elected to go for the Deming Prize until the completion of the examination, a twelve-month period, was nothing short of phenomenal. Preparing for the exam put intense pressure on all the various departments and divisions within the company and on all the officers as well, including myself. We found organizations in the company that weren't really up to speed in a totally comprehensive, integrated, and systemic way of providing customer satisfaction. At that time we began a series of intense management reviews, repeated over and over again, in which department heads and division vice presidents had to stand up time after time and go through what they were doing, how they were doing it, what results they were getting, and what their future plans and problems were—all supported with data and analysis. During these reviews, each presenter had his or her top managers and staff there as backup and to listen to the answers. As this process continued, we began to realize that about one-third of the departments in the General Office and maybe an equal proportion of divisions within the company still had gaps in their programs or were not perfectly aligned with our corporate goals. By repeatedly going through the process in practice for the Deming exam, all of those departments ultimately got up to speed and rose to the level of the very best of the departments. We had been told by other Deming Prize winners that this is what would happen as we prepared ourselves for the Deming Prize audits, and it is exactly why we decided to challenge for the prize.

Top management also realized that there were still numerous gaps in our own thinking as we worked our way through this period. We began to recognize additional improvement opportunities, and we came to see that at best we had achieved no more than half of our potential and that enormous gains could still be made, even though we were at the stage of going for the Deming Prize. Our eyes have now been opened to the fact that the opportunities for improvement are literally endless. It was as if we had just been gathering the low-hanging fruit from a tree. When we looked up, we could see much more fruit hanging on even higher and higher branches. But until we faced the trial of getting ready for the exam, we weren't able to see those opportunities; we weren't able to recognize many problems that needed work. I am sometimes asked whether I would have elected to challenge for the Deming Prize, if I had known before what I know now. My somewhat thoughtful answer is yes. It is not something to be entered into casually, but the improvement and gains obtained thereby are too great to forego. If you truly respect your company and its people, there is no other option than to challenge them to be the best. The way we chose to do this was through the Deming Prize process.

At FPL, not only top management, but people throughout the organization are constantly recognizing problems that previously would have just been overlooked or accepted as part of the sys-

tem. Now that the manner in which problems can be corrected and solved is available and understood, it is as if a whole new world has appeared. Suddenly all those problems become visible, and throughout the entire organization we have increased our level of expectations and realize that there are all manner of additional improvements that can and should be made. If anything, we are not even half-way there. And by the time FPL's people correct what they see now, the situation will have changed and there will be even more opportunities for continued effort. It is enormously satisfying to our employees to take on and solve one problem after another. Indeed, as is said so often, quality improvement is not a destination; it's a journey, and the trip can be very enjoyable.

So, the second main thing we learned is that to put a complete quality management system in place requires the full commitment of top management. This means not only visible leadership and participation, but of greater importance, the commitment to change. The most profound change that may need to be made is a willingness to trust every one of the company's employees: to come to realize that they can and will do an outstanding job of managing their own work if given the proper leadership and training. Only when you have top management sending a clear and consistent message of their commitment will other employees be willing to make TQM work.

If you are in the middle management of a company that is somewhere in this spectrum of improving quality, you should be constantly pushing those above you to get even more deeply involved in the entire process. You might be surprised at just how effective your suggestion could be. Top management might be holding back out of concern that the middle management of the company might not support a greater effort in quality improvement, but if they learn that those who would have to do most of

the work are eager to get started, you might find that the top management of the company is very receptive to your input.

If you are in top management, you need to find out what the total, comprehensive quality improvement management system is all about and how it should be installed in your own company. I am convinced that the Japanese have come up with such a system and that it works. Many companies throughout the United States badly need to get started with their own quality improvement efforts.

Some American managers seem troubled by finding that we can learn from the Japanese. I have no such problem. The world is getting smaller and we all need to learn from each other. Our eyes have been opened in ways that we never imagined when we took that first trip to Japan in 1984.

As I see the progress that is being made and the heightened interest being shown in total quality management by American companies, I am greatly encouraged. They may be at different stages of implementation, but they are moving in the right direction.

If what I have said so far has not frightened you, then it is time to read on and learn how we went about installing TQM at FPL.

# The Voice of the Customer

*F*requently when I make a speech on quality I tell the old joke about three men sentenced to be executed who were given one last request. The Frenchman said that he would like to have a bottle of fine French wine to drink before he was executed. The Japanese answered that as a world-class expert on quality, he would like to give his famous speech on the subject one more time. The American requested that he be executed before the Japanese so that he would not have to listen to any more speeches on quality. Since my audience knows they are about to hear another speech on quality, it still draws a good laugh. (I am told that prisoners appreciate gallows humor.) Several lessons, however, can be drawn from this little story.

First, if you have large amounts of patience and time and are willing to spend a lifetime learning how, you can make a few high-quality products in the manner of the skilled craftsman, like the French winemaker. If, on the other hand, you want to mass-produce large volumes of high-quality consumer products, you can become quite successful like the Japanese, improve your own and other people's lifestyles, and become very rich in the process. If this is your goal, you need a management system that provides a process by which large numbers of people can work together to achieve a very high-level common purpose. If you are about to die in a few minutes, maybe you don't need to worry anymore about the competition or quality, but if you intend to stay in business and prosper in today's and tomorrow's environment, you had better be very much aware of what is happening with your competitors all over the world, especially what they are doing with quality.

When Americans think about quality management, the thing that comes to mind most often is employee participation in quality circles. While QC circles are very important, they are not the most important part of the system. Today, the Japanese say that quality circles are only about 20 percent of the total quality system. The most important element is policy management, or policy deployment as it is sometimes called.

Through the process of policy management the "voice of the customer" is heard, interpreted, and converted into positive action. It is through policy management that top management provides policy direction to the entire organization on what is important if the company is to achieve customer satisfaction. How is this different from business strategy as practiced in the United States? As I see it, the principal difference is the strong focus on customer satisfaction as the central theme of the process. Customer satisfaction is based on what the customer says as determined by surveys, and is followed up with the extreme attention to detail and thoroughness so typical of the Japanese—not so much a matter of *what* is done, but rather *how* it is done.

The Japanese survey their customers over and over. Then they stratify the customers in a different manner and resurvey them. Management personally goes out and talks to the customer. Then they go back to speak with people whom they lost as customers, to find out what the competition did better and why they lost the sale. Then they do it all over again. In Japan there is a sort of national joke about the vast number of customer surveys that take place, to the point that everyone seems to be surveying each other. Anyone who has ever bought a Honda automobile may remember receiving, over a two-year or longer period, a number of successive questionnaires on how well the car is working, whether there is a way for Honda to improve, and so on.

Florida Power & Light defines quality as meeting the needs, expectations, and desires of its customers. But by itself that statement doesn't mean much. It is only when these needs become identified, prioritized, and converted into goals that anything can be done about them. This process begins with customer surveys. Our first formal customer survey was taken in 1985, and it was not very sophisticated. It was a rather simple man-on-the-street affair. It did have the virtue of being quick, and it was a good learning experience for us. And it did at least give us a baseline from which to start.

Our counselors, who started working with us in 1985, had been pressing us for data on our customers' needs and wants. Our response was to say that we knew what our customers wanted. From even this first survey's results, however, we learned that we did not know as much about our customers as we thought we knew. For example, we now place a higher importance on public safety than we had before the surveys. We did not consider that this was as large an issue in the minds of our customers as the surveys told us it was.

Each time we repeated this process, our results became more scientific and more precise. Today, while FPL does some of its own surveys, they also employ professionals for the more complex ones. In the beginning, the company surveyed residential customers only, but now it also covers commercial and industrial customers. And it interviews various other groups who are considered to be indirect customers, groups who in one way or another speak for the customer. Once the customers' needs, or the voice of the customer, are understood, then management can begin to develop a hierarchy of customer requirements that need to be addressed. At FPL this is done primarily through what is called the "Table of Tables," a matrix that cross-relates customer requirements and specific quality elements. We borrowed heavily from Dr. Yoji Akao's work on "quality function deployment" in this area.

There are ten steps in our process of generating the Table of Tables—from identifying the customers to ranking the quality elements. First, we decide who the customers are. Separating the rate-paying customers into residential, commercial/industrial, and wholesale groups is not too hard. This is the traditional way we have thought about classes of electric customers. But today we go further and look at subgroups of these customers. For example, the needs of a residential customer in a high-rise condominium in South Florida are not the same as those of a rural, residential customer in North Florida. Likewise, a shopping mall does not have the same requirements as a hospital, and so on. After identifying major customer groups, the next step is to survey the customers to obtain data on their requirements. When we first did this, we identified seventy different direct customer needs. Again, direct customer surveys are developed and conducted both inhouse and by outside professionals. In addition, for smaller customer groups we use both focus groups and direct face-to-face interviews.

Then there are the indirect customers—those organizations that represent and speak for the customer, such as the Nuclear Regulatory Commission and the Florida Public Service Commission. For the indirect customers, we annually review all of the codes and regulations with the staffs of the different regulatory bodies to be sure we understand both the letter and spirit of the law. Altogether, fifty-six indirect customer needs have been identified.

Based on the survey results, the needs are weighted for importance and then grouped into nineteen quality elements. These elements include items like courteous customer service, continuity of service, price, and environmental protection. Next we start to determine the relationship between the voice of the customer and FPL activities.

At this point the different customer groups are weighted based on their size and electric usage. This weighting is then applied to rank the importance of the nineteen quality elements. Direct and indirect quality elements are combined, and then we arrive at the overall ranking of the quality elements.

Finally, we are ready and able to prioritize FPL activities based on what quality elements the customers told us were most important to them. When this process is complete it is summarized on one large sheet of paper—the Table of Tables mentioned above. The entire process I have just described is what we call listening to the voice of the customer. The Japanese call it the market-in approach.

All of this may sound somewhat complex, but then this process has been developed for FPL's unique set of circumstances and has been modified and fine-tuned over a number of years. For the more technical part of this process, we in management have used staff support.

It doesn't have to be all that difficult and complex; in fact, it can be quite simple. If I were managing an auto repair shop, for example, I would just talk to my customers; make a simple ranking of their views on our keeping commitments in price, schedule, and results; place their views in priority; measure the current situation; and set improvement targets. It can be that simple and still be effective. We have been told—and I believe it is true—that the smaller the organization, the easier it is to do all this.

Once the customers' wants have been determined as factually as possible, the policy-setting management group must get together to look at data on customer needs and wants, and use the data to develop a few important objectives for the organization. These objectives must be detailed and must focus specifically on those things that are important for the company to do well, from the customer's point of view—in other words, on what the company needs to do to achieve greater customer satisfaction than the competition. Management must also select the quality measurements that will be used and the goals to be obtained—goals specific as to what and when. Every company or even every product line of each company meets different needs; therefore, each company must work this through for itself, with its own customers' needs and its own business environment in mind. The essential thing is that the customers' wants are determined as factually as possible.

FPL also communicates the voice of the customer, as expressed by the Table of Tables, to all its employees (see Figure 4.1). It is sent to every work location with instructions that it be placed on the wall next to the bulletin boards. This is done so that every employee can see what our customers think is important.

This entire process of focusing on customers' requirements is analyzed and repeated as often as necessary. In FPL's case, this has been once each year.

If the management of the airline on which my wife and I flew back from Europe had been out talking with their customers, they could have developed a nice list of problems to work on—but then they may prefer not to hear how they are doing. They may

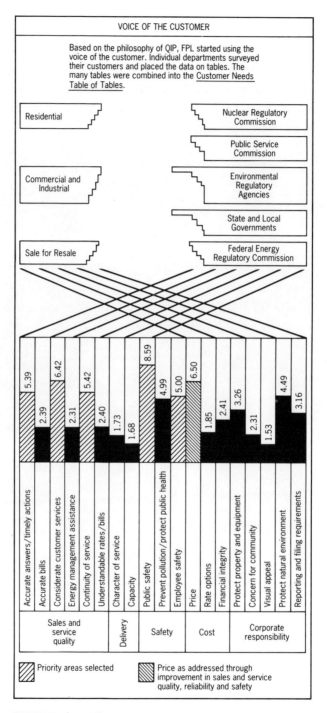

**FIGURE 4.1 The Customer Needs Table of Tables cross-relates customer requirements and specific quality elements.**

be more comfortable that way. If this is true, they are not so different from the management of many other companies. But there is a better way, and ultimately the airline that perfects it is going to be very successful.

# Policy Management:
# Doing the Right Thing

*I*n 1985, at one of my early meetings with our lead counselor, Dr. Asaka, he made the point that all the elements of Japan's quality management system contribute to the overall results and reinforce each other, but that policy management is the most important single element. Policy management is the TQM system element he stressed in teaching us. Moreover, in his view, this was the most desirable place for a company to start implementing the system. The fact that FPL already had quality improvement teams was not a significant problem; in fact, Dr. Asaka said that most companies start with teams. However, he felt that ideally management should first decide on the direction the organization should be going, and then send loud, clear signals to every employee so that all quality improvement efforts, including team activities, will be focused from the very start. Policy management, or as it is sometimes called policy deployment, is the top-down strategic use of quality to achieve greater corporate health.

As I have already mentioned, the first and second principles of Florida Power & Light's quality system are *satisfy the customer* and *speak with facts.* The third principle of the system is *PDCA,* or plan-do-check-act, the well-known Deming cycle. It was the repeated use of this third principle that allowed us to implement our corporate policy objectives and develop such a clear understanding of our capabilities for improvement.

Any organization that has existed for any length of time is probably good at "plan-do"; at FPL we had always done a pretty good job of this. But back in 1985 the "check-act" part was virtually nonexistent. "Check-act," as we came to learn it, means using data to analyze whether the actual results of "do" were the ones planned, and then taking action to improve the next PDCA cycle. (At that time we would have said we did this, but in hindsight it is clear that any attempts we made were pretty superficial.) And PDCA is applied not only to improve problem-solving skills but also to improve the quality improvement process itself; this application is probably the most important use of the PDCA cycle.

Dr. Asaka likened a company just getting started to a group of arrows dropped on the floor randomly, pointing in all directions. The arrows represent the efforts of the different departments—forceful and well intentioned, but uncoordinated. After the first attempt at policy deployment (that is, the first PDCA cycle), the arrows look like the spokes of a hand-held fan, more or less pointing in the same general direction but still not perfectly aligned. After another iteration of the PDCA cycle, the arrows are parallel and all point in the same direction but have gaps between them. Finally, after one more turn of the PDCA wheel, the arrows are all aligned in a bundle, mutually supporting each other, with a third dimension, or depth. The arrows in the bundle support each other and produce greatly enhanced strength. Likewise, in an organization, the various elements of the company work together cross-functionally to produce greatly enhanced results. Today I use this same description to explain the effects of policy management at FPL.

After this third stage is attained, enormous energy is focused on those very few issues that are most important to achieving customer satisfaction. Ultimately everyone in the company needs to understand and work to achieve these common objectives, but it is the responsibility of top management to lead the company through the successive stages of this process. No one else can do it.

Dr. Asaka went on to say that a company with 500 employees or less could complete the implementation of the total quality management process in as little as one year but that a company like FPL, with 15,000 employees, would typically need three years, even if we were very dedicated and determined in our efforts. As it worked out, his timing estimate was accurate, and I can see how it could easily have taken even longer.

The starting point for policy management is to listen to the voice of the customer. As we began to obtain more useful customer survey data and to understand our customers better, we learned much more about our own capabilities for making improvement. Our priority-setting abilities became more precise, our goal-setting skills more scientific, and our ability to create a hierarchy of customer needs and wants improved.

One of our early mistakes in policy management was a common one: we tried to work on too many things at once. The first time we went through the process, if someone suggested dropping an item from the quality element (customer requirements) list, they were looked at as if they were proposing murder. Our counselors' way of putting it was that we were chasing too many rabbits at the same time. Eventually we narrowed down the number of things designated for major improvements to just the vital few. In 1989, there were only eight elements on the list for the entire organization.

1. Reduce customer dissatisfaction
2. Increase customer satisfaction

3. Reduce service unavailability
4. Reduce transmission forced outages
5. Increase nuclear availability
6. Reduce fossil forced outages
7. Improve nuclear safety
8. Improve employee safety

Moreover, any given department would only work on about three of these at the same time.

All the important quality elements should ultimately be addressed, but it is also important to concentrate on improving only a few at a time, starting with the ones most important to the customer. This selection process demands all the skill and judgment management can muster. Enormous energy will be spent on improving these few most important goals; obviously they need to be the proper ones. "Doing the right thing" is what it's all about. (You probably don't want to direct your company to make the best horse-drawn wagons in the world.)

To help illustrate what such goals might be, here are two currently used at FPL, as derived from what our customers told us they want. The first is to improve the reliability of electricity service by reducing the average number of minutes without electricity per customer per year from 41 in 1989, to 38 in 1990, and to 33 in 1991. The second is to improve customer satisfaction by reducing the number of customer complaints per 1,000 customers from 0.25 in 1989, to 0.2 in 1990, and to 0.15 in 1991. Besides representing the "right things" for FPL to do, these goals are also quite precise. But remember that at this time, FPL's understanding of exactly what must be done to meet goals like these is greatly improved over what it was in 1985 when we began to install our total quality management system. We continue to make improvements in the goal-setting process each time we go through the cycle.

Another early mistake we made was relying almost entirely on gut feeling and not nearly enough on data in priority setting. Too often the person with the strongest opinion or loudest voice decided the close ones, and I myself was absolutely one of the worst offenders. But as we began to obtain more accurate and useful data and to insist on speaking with facts, this became less and less true. Once we had learned to discipline ourselves in this manner, we were amazed at how much more we were able to accomplish in a much shorter time. We actually began to end meetings early, with much better communication and decisions having taken place. You certainly still need to exercise judgment, but judgment based on data—on facts—produces a better result.

Keep in mind the application of the quality management system improves communication throughout the organization. This process of speaking with facts using a common quality language is one of the major ancillary benefits of the process, and it is a phenomenon cited by most TQM companies. Our counselors kept insisting that we speak with facts and many of our presenters had some very embarrassing moments when they did not have any data at all to back up a statement. Our counselors forced us to become more skilled in both the use of data and the type of data we used. As a result, our ability to determine the root cause of problems to be overcome also improved steadily.

While setting the proper corporate goals to achieve customer satisfaction is necessary, it is not enough. For example, that FPL set an overall goal in 1989 of 41 minutes without electricity per customer per year is not very useful to the people out in the field. There is no way they can relate that number to what they do. And until the people out in the field start doing something differently, nothing has happened that will make anything improve.

In order to translate the corporate goal into specific activities, first the overall goal must be broken down into smaller pieces that apply to the work units. In this case each of FPL's five divisions is assigned its own piece of the overall goal. This is accomplished through a two-stage, back-and-forth negotiation with top management. The Japanese refer to this process as "catch ball." The divisional goals are not equal, but when they are all weighted and combined they add up to the corporate goal. For example, the goal for overall corporate improvement in this quality element was set at 11 minutes, or from 52 minutes in 1988 to 41 minutes in 1989. The Southeastern Division's piece of this corporate goal was a two-minute reduction.

To achieve this reduction, numerous specific projects must be identified, planned, and completed. The Southeastern Division collected data on the types and duration of interruptions in their area, then analyzed the data to determine the root causes of the interruptions. Various countermeasures to overcome these root problems were considered and ranked according to cost-benefit ratio and feasibility. In 1988, all of the projects needed to achieve the 1989 overall improvement were tentatively proposed for inclusion in the 1989 quality improvement plans.

In 1985, we created a committee to manage the policy deployment process. This policy deployment committee was made up of the top seven officers of the company; it is their responsibility to review all five divisions' reliability improvement proposals, select the best mix of projects for the company, and tentatively approve them. For example, in each of the five divisions, projects to reduce electric outages are included on the list.

At the same time, the policy deployment committee also reviews the projects proposed in each of the other areas targeted for major quality improvement and selects the best cost-benefit mix of projects for each one. By design, the policy deployment committee is made up of the same officers as the budget committee, so after they have selected the best mix of projects, they change hats and call in the financial department. Then the entire package of quality improvement projects is compared to the financial plan for the company and the next year's budget is set. At this point, the budget committee may elect to do even more, or they may have to cut back on the items in the quality improvement plan. Since the projects have already been ranked by cost-benefit ratio, the budget committee knows just which projects to add or subtract.

Obviously, this is a balancing act for the policy deployment/ budget committee. But then it probably is not very different from the way an ordinary household budget is prepared.

As the quality improvement plans and financial budgets are brought into agreement and jointly approved, it is also necessary to adjust the corporate quality targets and goals to reflect only those projects approved in the plan. It is essential to give the field the resources necessary to make the expected improvement. If this does not happen, the system loses creditability. The fact that the projects approved are the very ones that the divisions themselves have analyzed and proposed also strengthens the creditability of the system. The Southeastern Division came up with projects such as surveying and upgrading to standard the twelve feeders most affected by lightning interruptions—0.3 minutes improvement expected; reducing the load on overloaded laterals—0.2 minutes improvement expected; and so forth.

All in all, the Southeastern Division will need to engineer and work several hundred specific improvement projects to achieve their target of a two-minute reduction in service outages. But now the people on the spot know exactly what they are expected to do to support the customer satisfaction objective of improved service reliability.

Typically each work group plans projects in at least two and probably three elements slated for major quality improvement.

After the projects are completed, data are collected and analyzed to determine if the expected improvement has occurred. Lessons are learned through this check-act process, and then the cycle is repeated all over again the next year.

Policy management is an enormously powerful tool. I have seen companies make a tenfold improvement in such things as on-time delivery in as little as two years while simultaneously reducing lead time on deliveries to one-third of what they had been. One company I know of said its product reliability, as measured by total down time for repairs during the first year of operation, would become twice as good as its nearest competitor. It achieved a threefold overall improvement. Moreover, these were the very things their customers were saying were most important to them. These companies gained an enormous competitive advantage as a result of these improvements.

These results, however, don't happen just because of policy deployment. There are many other parts to the system, so the story doesn't stop here.

# *Quality Improvement Teams:*
# *Respect for People*

*E*ach November the Union of Japanese Scientists and Engineers (JUSE) sponsors a series of quality seminars and events leading up to the Deming Prize award ceremony. One of these seminars, the Foreman's Conference, takes place over a three-day period during which representatives from about forty-five different companies make presentations on their successful quality improvement efforts. All together about 500 people attend the conference. Three presentations are conducted simultaneously, and the audience for each is made up primarily of employees of those companies making presentations. Florida Power & Light is the only American organization to send a quality improvement (QI) team to this seminar for each of the last four years. And, of course, FPL's team is the only one who needs interpreters to translate their presentation into Japanese.

It is a great honor to be chosen to make a presentation at this conference. Needless to say, the teams are selected by their companies with great care. Accordingly, they present some of the best quality improvement stories in Japan. Florida Power & Light is not so different. Each year, as part of the team recognition process, we select the best twenty-eight teams in the company.

51

The team that goes to Japan to present their QI story is selected from this short list. I am told that their presentation is well received; I've also heard that it is the best attended of the conference, but in truth this is probably due more to curiosity than anything else. When they return to Florida the team members are always on cloud nine. After they have settled down and rested a little, they are sent around the company to tell other Quality Improvement Program (QIP) teams about their experience and what they learned.

Today FPL has 1,600 teams in operation, and they compete for the opportunity to present their quality improvement story at conferences in the United States and/or the Foreman's Conference in Japan. This internal competition and recognition process has been a major contributor to our teams' overall improvement. The quality of most of our teams' work is now at a high level, but this was not always the case.

The company formed its first four pilot QI teams in 1981. After about four months, we evaluated the results of these four teams and decided to go forward with a companywide program of quality improvement teams. By the end of 1982, seventy teams were functioning. Initially we trained the team leaders in only three of the seven basic tools of problem solving: check sheets, Pareto diagrams, and graphs. A group of team facilitators received some additional, advanced training in the problem-solving process and in small-group dynamics. Typically, each facilitator was used as an expert resource by about six to ten teams. Participation on teams was voluntary, and the teams were free to select any problem they wanted to work on.

Overseeing the entire program was a newly created quality council made up of about twenty vice presidents and department heads and chaired by FPL's chairman. The quality council acted as a clearinghouse for information. At its monthly four-hour meeting, case studies of quality improvement successes were shared, overall results and problems were discussed, and future short-range plans were formulated. In those early days this council meeting was the focal point for all our quality improvement efforts. It served its purpose well, but at this time, it was narrowly directed toward increasing the number of teams and improving their performance.

At about this time we also organized a Quality Improvement Department, which was under the direction of one of our early proponents of quality improvement, Kent Sterett. From the start this department was deliberately kept small. It did not have any line or supervisory responsibilities, but rather was used to coordinate and standardize quality improvement processes. It provided staff support to the quality council, assisted in developing quality improvement training programs, maintained records on the program, and administered the team recognition program. Ultimately, it became the interface with both our Japanese counselors and all other organizations outside the company.

Typically, quality improvement teams were expected to meet for about one hour a week; for this activity they did not report to their manager but de facto to their facilitator and the quality council. As might be expected, since participation on teams was voluntary, the team members were generally very enthusiastic. This was something new and different for the company. The team members were being asked to use their heads for a change. During the first year, about half of the teams learned to use the process well, produced practical solutions, and obtained good results. This success gave management the necessary encouragement to keep the program going. However, as we quickly learned, there were many problems with our initial approach. But, then, we had to start somewhere. As long as you are willing to be self-critical and make periodic improvements based on experience, it is better to go ahead and get started. If you wait until you have the perfect system, you will never get started.

One of the lessons we learned in those early days was that some of the teams started in on very large, complex, company-wide problems—multifaceted problems that were far beyond the teams' abilities. To be properly analyzed these problems required the input of data from several departments, and even more critically, implementing whatever corrective action was called for required the close cooperation of the other departments. Since implementation would have to be across functional lines of the organization, it would also require approval at a very high level. Naturally, then, these teams ran into difficulty and bogged down or they came up with solutions that had no real value. Then when nothing changed for the better, there was finger pointing and we were right back at square one. Fortunately, only a small number of teams followed this path.

To overcome this problem, in early 1984 we divided the problem-solving teams into two types. Functional teams, which today make up approximately 80 percent of the total number of problem-solving teams, work on strictly local problems for which they can implement improvements themselves. They are typically made up of about six people who continue to be volunteers. These teams are standing in nature and work on one problem after another.

Task teams, which comprise the other 20 percent, are appointed by management to work on the more difficult and complex problems that are generally cross-functional in nature. These teams are ad hoc and disband after each problem is solved. The members frequently include both staff and professional employees. Since they are working on problems chosen by management and the members have been selected for the team because of their skills and knowledge, they are not considered volunteers.

We established a third type of team in 1985—not a problem-solving team but rather a lead team made up of the supervisors and managers at a work site or department. Its function is to oversee all QIP activities in the department, including the functional teams.

Another problem we experienced with QI teams in the early days was the feeling of the middle managers and supervisors that they had no part in the process and their consequent lack of support of it. In fact, many tended to regard the whole thing as interfering with "regular" work. At this time managers were being measured in the same way they had always been, mainly by the productivity indexes of standard industrial engineering. As we know, the squeaking wheel gets the grease, and from the managers' point of view, these productivity indexes were the squeaking wheels. Since team activity was a highly visible use of the employees' time and represented time taken away from "regular" work, it was naturally resented. Of course, the team members could care less, and this added to the friction.

Nevertheless, by 1984 when we made our first trip to Japan, we had 700 teams operating. Our functional teams had begun to work on simpler, more localized problems and were producing solutions that could generally be implemented locally. Through training and practice they were beginning to become skilled in the use of the basic tools of problem solving. The task teams also were becoming more adept at problem solving, and we had seen a few breakthrough improvements. In fact, we were starting to see a lot of improvement and were feeling pretty smug about our QIP.

At that time, because most of us thought that quality improvement team activity was the entire system, we thought we had in place an excellent quality improvement program. Our bubble burst on that first trip to Japan when we saw many quality circles that were much more effective than even our best team. But what was far more important, we also saw that the quality management system was much more than just teams.

We came back to Florida with the knowledge that we had a very long way to go. A major effort was undertaken both to train the supervisors in QIP and to enable them to act as the facilitator for their own teams. Also, we realized that the supervisors should be measured by different standards that included time spent on team activities and the supervisor's support of teams. It is important that the supervisor/facilitator provide the necessary support in terms of a time and place to meet, encouragement, and recognition. The supervisor should give the teams a little guidance but needs to be careful not to dominate. Today many of the teams have adopted the practice of getting the concurrence of their supervisor on the problem they are going to work on. Although this is not mandatory, it does result in the supervisor buying in from the start. Also, it makes for a greater sense of team spirit since everyone is working on the same agenda.

The company influences the problems being worked on in another way. A key word file was established in the quality improvement department. Before teams select a problem, they check this file to learn what other teams have already done. As a result, if a team elects to work on a problem that is the same as or similar to one addressed by another team, they will have at least thought through why they are doing so and what they are going to do differently. When this happens, almost without exception the solutions complement each other and produce a better overall result.

Today FPL teaches all its employees the use of the seven basic tools of problem solving. Since these tools are widely discussed in quality literature, I am not going to cover them in depth, but I will list them here:

1. *Check sheets,* which are used by the teams to gather data.
2. *Histograms,* which are used in statistical quality control applications and to help understand the distribution of data.
3. *Pareto diagrams,* which are used to differentiate the significant elements of a problem from the less significant ones.
4. *Cause and effect diagrams,* which help identify and analyze the root cause of a problem. (These are especially useful in conjunction with Pareto diagrams.)
5. *Graphs,* which display data over time and help show trends.
6. *Scatter diagrams,* which display relationships between sets of data.
7. *Control charts,* which are used to track the variation of a process and to determine whether or not the process is in control.

One reason it takes so long to implement quality improvement completely throughout a large organization is that these tools must be taught to and understood by all team members. Team members really don't understand the power of these tools until they have successfully applied them in solving their own problems. For this reason, our training stresses the use of the tools in team problem solving. Sometimes this causes problems when the teams inappropriately apply a tool in an attempt to please management by using all seven tools. However, through practice, the teams learn when and how to use these problem-solving tools properly.

In some ways management itself is a bigger problem; they, after all, have been successful at solving problems all their lives without using these analytical tools. They must come to understand two things: One, if they are so good at managing and eliminating problems, why are all these problems still around? And two, the whole idea is to involve everyone in the problem-solving process, not just the managers. When this kind of participation happens, the annoying everyday problems are eliminated by the employees themselves on a day-to-day basis. Managers don't even know about most of these problems, and they wouldn't have enough time to work on all of them even if they did. At this point in the process the employees take responsibility for and manage their own activities. In part, this is what we are talking about when we say that the fourth principle of QIP is respect for people.

Here is a good example of how this works. We knew that it took longer than we liked to answer some of our customers' questions at one of our regional telephone centers. A functional team decided to work on this problem. Their data quickly told them that the major part of the problem was those calls that required some research to obtain the correct answer. Specifically, this type of phone request was taking 623 minutes to complete. The team conducted a survey of about 100 customers; the survey told them that the customer expected and would be satisfied with a 60–minute delay in getting an answer. Since the phone center was also very busy with other, more straightforward phone calls as well, most of the delay was occurring before the employee could get free to do the necessary research. The countermeasure proposed by the team was to free up one customer representative to do the research and complete all calls of this type.

When this presentation was made to the department's lead team, they shook their heads. "You mean to say that at times the center is overloaded with work and your solution to the problem is to take away one of the telephone representatives?" The proposal flew in the face of experience and common sense. But the members of the lead team could find no flaw in the team's analysis or logic, and by this time they had faith in the process and respect for their people. They said, "Go ahead and do it, and let's see the results."

The results were just as the team had predicted. Calls requiring research were now completed in only 47 minutes. Moreover, the overall efficiency improved and the phone center gained the equivalent productivity of one additional employee. As a result, the more routine calls were also answered faster.

The lesson is that the process and respect for people produced this result. This kind of improvement would not have happened at FPL a few years earlier. When the supervisors detected an overload of work, they would have added an additional employee. Instead, with the assistance of their employees—the ones who know the most about the problem in the department—they were able to do a better job of satisfying their customers without bringing in any more staff. Respect for people is an important principle.

Only after employees have begun to manage their own work can managers spend their time on the more important issues that need to be addressed but for which they never have had enough time—things like improving the long-range effectiveness of their department, for example. Also at this stage, they can and should take great pride in their employees' day-to-day quality improvement successes.

When they are just getting started many managers say, "I am overworked now. I just don't have any more time in the day." And they ask, "How much time is this going to take?" This is the wrong question. A better question for them to start with is, "What am I spending my time on—fire fighting or preventing fires?" This management system permits you to spend your time on the right things—upstream control of problems, not just coping with their effects.

In addition to the seven tools, we also teach a problem-solving method we call the quality improvement story. This method is the one taught by the Union of Japanese Scientists and Engineers (JUSE). Some version of it seems to be used by all the companies in Japan who apply total quality control (TQC) principles. We adapted it to our own situation and implemented it across the company.

The principal purpose of this method is to force a systematic and logical approach to problem solving. When we found a team bogged down and not making progress, we went back over the steps they had supposedly completed. Almost always, somewhere in the process one of the steps had been left out or done improperly. When this step was redone correctly, the team began to move forward again.

Just as in the use of the seven tools, in the beginning we also insisted that the problem-solving process be used. The teams may at times have felt they were using a cannon to kill a fly, but we learned that if the teams didn't utilize all of the steps, they generally didn't produce very good solutions.

The seven steps in the problem-solving process are:

1. *Reason for improvement:* What seems to be the problem?
2. *Current situation:* Where are we now?
3. *Analysis:* What are the root causes of the problem?
4. *Countermeasures:* What should we do to improve the situation?
5. *Results:* What happened as a result of our actions?
6. *Standardization:* How do we hold on to the improvement?
7. *Future plans:* What is the next item we need to work on to achieve further improvement in this area?

Now that most of our teams are proficient in the use of the quality improvement story and the seven problem-solving tools, not as much insistence is placed on the strict use of these steps in the problem-solving process.

We have found that as employees become more at ease with this problem-solving process, they expand the use of it to their other everyday activities. As a result, everyone is thinking about their customers and how to improve at all times. For example, one of the results of this changed way of thinking is a better suggestion program.

The benefits of all this effort are enormous. Normally, it takes a team about six months to solve a problem and implement corrective action. The description of the team's entire seven-step process is called a QI (quality improvement) story. The use of the standard QI story format improves and speeds up communications. The part of the story that describes what was and will be done is called an Improvement Action Memo (IAM). Some of the teams have now completed ten, and in a few cases twenty, IAMs. The improvements are all over the company. One of my favorite early ones was the team in the mailroom that reduced misaddressed mail by 98 percent. Or there is the team whose department was responsible for collecting about $50 million a year. Seventy-one percent of this revenue was delayed getting into the bank by one or more days. They have reduced that delay so that now 96 percent of all deposits are made on the same day they are received.

It works the other way too. We were very bad about paying our vendors on time. This wasn't due to any policy but rather to weak administration. A team in the accounts payable department worked on this problem and improved the on-time payment of bills from 76 percent to 93 percent.

The team that went to Japan in 1989 was from one of the power plants, and was made up largely of welders. They perfected a new and much better method to x-ray boiler tubes to detect weak spots in the tubes before they fail. The steam to drive the turbine is produced inside these tubes. A major leak in even one tube requires that the plant be shut down until the tube is repaired. The result of the new x-ray technique has been greatly reduced boiler tube failures. This team's idea will make a major improvement in the quality goal of reducing the forced outage rate of their power plant. It also will produce about $65,000 annual savings for their plant.

A word is in order here about replication—the process of taking one team's solution and utilizing it elsewhere in the company. The improved method of x-raying tubes, for example, can also be used in nine other plants. This means that the benefits of this improvement are ten times more than they would be if they were only used at the one plant. Needless to say, there must be a system in place to make this happen. And remember, FPL has 1,600 teams functioning, cleaning up one problem after another. When all these improvements are multiplied by replication, the overall improvement is mind-boggling.

As I have said, one of the major benefits of a companywide application of the QI story is that there is a common language used across the organization. People from any part of the company can follow the logic of a quality improvement story even if they are unfamiliar with the details of the problem. This common language, this practical application of the motto "speak with facts," improves communication enormously. It is difficult to fathom how important an improvement this is until you see it in action.

I attended a quality management seminar at Xerox (a 1989 Baldrige winner) recently, at which this same point was being made. Communication in their company had been improved dramatically by the use of data and the common language of quality. Xerox employees from many different nations who literally spoke different languages could now communicate with each other better than ever before through the language of quality. Perhaps, like the common languages of mathematics and music, the language of quality will help make the world a better place.

Today many people from other organizations, both within the United States and from other parts of the world, visit FPL. Generally, FPL arranges for guests to see a team QI story presentation. The only request made of the team chosen for this task is that their story be complete, including a solution, results, standardization, and future plans. Otherwise, the FPL coordinators just grab the first team that is readily available. Literally hundreds of teams have made presentations to visiting groups. Visitors are always impressed with the teams' skill in both using and analyzing data. Although the visitors don't come right out and say so, we can tell from their comments that they think we have shown them our very best team, maybe even the one that was chosen to go to Japan!

A by-product of having all these teams make presentations is that a large number of people become quite skilled at standing and talking before an audience. This is a very good way to improve employees' public-speaking skills.

Another frequent reaction of visitors to team presentations is: "Big deal. That little problem doesn't need all of this effort to solve." This kind of reaction most often comes from high-level managers. My response is that of course there are people in the audience who could have solved the problem themselves in less time, but time as such is not the point. Not everyone is a vice president with their experience or salary. Our aim is to help everyone throughout the company perform at very high levels and to let them take ownership of one activity after another—in fact, to let them become the managers of their own work.

A company that is organized and managed in this way is going to get the best out of all its people. Total quality management will afford it great efficiency and strength, and thereby a big competitive advantage.

# *Quality in Daily Work: Doing Things Right*

$Q$uality in Daily Work (QIDW) is managing with a capital "M". It is attention to every detail of every step of everything one does. It is why the gardens in Japan are so exquisite. It is why in a Japanese hotel when you arrive in your room the flowers are fresh, hot tea awaits you, and your luggage is already there. It is why the trains run on time. QIDW is doing things right the first time and every time. QIDW is a major element in meeting customers' needs, wants, and desires.

Let me use another personal anecdote here: recently I went to one of our local hospitals for some tests. I arrived at the appointed time and was met by a pleasant hospital employee who personally escorted me to the lab. There I was introduced to a very efficient technician who was waiting for me with all the necessary equipment at hand, all properly laid out. So far, so good. Then things began to fall apart. It seemed that I needed an I.V. line. The person scheduled to do this was not there. The technician called for a resident who, when contacted, said that it wasn't her job. A second resident was paged three times without response. Then several other departments were contacted, all to no avail. Finally, after a lot of complaining to a supervisor that this was the third day they had had this exact same problem that week, someone did show up to administer the I.V., but 45 minutes late. I was thinking, what this place needs is a little, not a lot but a little, quality in daily work. Most things were set up very well but one glitch ruined the schedule for an entire department for the rest of the day and for the third day that week. And it sure made a very poor impression on their customer, me.

I could use a hundred other examples of where QIDW is needed. And I am sure everyone could quickly make up their own list without even trying. We see these examples everywhere and everyday.

Quality in daily work is the method used to smooth out all the little problems that have such a negative impact on repetitive and routine operations. It takes all the sand out of the gears. And once you understand, it is so easy to do. I am convinced that employees everywhere want to do quality work. Then why don't they? Management is the problem.

By the time we introduced QIDW at Florida Power & Light in 1986, we had been using policy management for a year, so our people knew the goals the company had set for itself, that is, those things we needed to do well to achieve customer satisfaction. Also, by that time quality improvement teams had been functioning for five years. Again, this meant that our employees knew how to use the problem-solving process and its tools.

Therefore, early in 1986, I believed we were ready for the next step and I proudly, and with great fanfare, announced Quality in Daily Work (QIDW) to our people. Only later did I learn that the word "daily" caused a lot of confusion. Some of our employees and all of our Japanese counselors took the word literally: *daily,* not hourly or weekly or any other time period. But by then we were stuck with Quality in Daily Work and had to work very hard to explain that what Hudiburg really meant was all repetitive, cyclical, or routine work, regardless of how often it took place. As QIDW concentrates on controlling and improving the process of routine activities, it promotes standardization of processes so that good results can be maintained and systematically improved.

The first step in implementing QIDW was to explain the concept of internal customers: the internal customer is the next person or department in a process. We asked our managers, and later all our employees, to look at their outputs to determine who uses them and how. Who are their customers? What do they do for their internal customers? What is the most important thing they do and what is the order of importance of the other things they do? What measurements do they use to know how they are doing? Finally, what is the most important thing they do that is most out of control?

After they had analyzed their own activities in this manner, we asked that they contact the internal customer of the most important thing that was most out of control and negotiate a quality standard of performance. Once standards are set and agreed upon, the next steps are flow charting the process used to meet their customers' needs, establishing targets and measurements in the process, and then assigning responsibilities for the proper operation of the control system.

This process really isn't as hard or as involved as it may sound. I remember going to a power plant for a review of their quality activities and hearing the clerks in the office describe their first QIDW success. They had identified four things they did as the most important ones. Of the four, the item that was most out of control was the receiving reports, records of the receipt of goods or services by the plant. After these reports were processed by the clerks at the plant, they were sent to accounts payable in the treasury department for vendor payment. The power plant clerks knew from an error report that they were making about twelve errors a week in the receiving reports.

One of the plant clerks called up their internal customer, a clerk in accounts payable. This was still a new idea to the treasury employee and required a little explaining. When the power plant clerk asked the treasury clerk what an acceptable error rate for receiving reports would be, she was told "Zero." The power plant clerk responded, "We aren't that good yet." They eventually negotiated a standard of no more than four errors a week for the receiving reports.

The power plant office flow charted the receiving report process, developed a check sheet for themselves, and did a little training with the guy down on the receiving dock on how to fill out a receiving report. None of this was very complex; moreover, the clerks did it all themselves.

The results, which they proudly showed me, were no more than four errors per week over a three-month period, a threefold improvement. Later their manager called me to report a zero-error record over a four-week period. I was very proud of them. Also, they had proved to me that the process of QIDW could work at FPL. Of course, that was only their initial control system. Since then these clerks have installed two more QIDW systems.

I think a word might be appropriate here about mutual support and encouragement. When I would get discouraged about some stupid thing I had done that had caused problems for the organization, I would get out of the office for a while. If I only had an hour or so, I would just wander into one of the General Office departments and start asking anyone I met to show me what they were doing in quality improvement. Better yet, if I had more time, I would arrange to spend a day with one of the line organizations and ask the same question. I never once failed to become inspired about what our people were doing. They were so excited and quick to show what they had been able to do. They were taking on chronic problems and making big improvements, and they knew it. Also, they knew exactly how they had done it and what they were going to do next. In the most profound way, they were the leaders. I always returned determined more than ever not to let them down.

By 1989 over 3,000 QIDW control systems were in operation at FPL. One activity after another had been stabilized and brought under control. Some are small systems; like the one at the power plant to reduce errors in receiving reports or one at another power plant that had reduced the percentage of times employees could not find the correct form in their stationery supply room from 10 percent to 1 percent. These localized systems address only a small part of a larger process, but the results all add up to a very big improvement in efficiency. Also, it sure does make coming to work more satisfying.

There are also some midsize QIDW systems, like the one in general engineering that controls the time to administratively process construction tracings and drawings to a maximum of seven days. Before QIDW was in place, this process took up to forty-five days. In talking to their internal customers, the general engineering department identified two problems: first, the processing of tracings and drawings just took too long; and second, their internal customer wasn't able to plan activities because the process was so variable and unpredictable.

To attack these problems the team used the QIP problem-solving process. They employed statistical process control (SPC) techniques and also relied heavily on flow charts. As a result of their analysis, they set a goal of not only reducing the average and maximum times to process their work, but also making a major improvement in the variability of this activity. Today the average processing time is four days and the variation is also now under control. The general engineering department's internal customers are now satisfied.

Some of the 3,000 QIDW control systems are very large, companywide systems, which may involve as many as seven different departments. It was just such a large QIDW system that reduced customer billing errors by over 80 percent.

Receiving accurate bills from the company is one of the nineteen items customers told us was important to them, but it is not one of the eight most important ones targeted for major improvement through policy deployment. The principal reason why this issue is of lesser priority to the customer is, most likely, that FPL has a good record of performance in this area. This makes the issue a perfect candidate for QIDW.

A large number of people are involved in producing an accurate bill. Probably 50 percent of all FPL's employees are part of the process. A list of only the major departments whose work must be correct illustrates the point: customer service (who open and close accounts), the distribution department (who set and remove meters), the meter test department, meter readers, computer programmers, computer operations, the bill-processing group, and the mailroom.

Each department flow charted its part of the process and set up its own control systems. After each departmental system was working reasonably well, a cross-functional team was formed to create an overall system for the entire process. Everyone's efforts were thereby integrated to produce the overall result desired. At one point, the bill-processing group realized that the format of the bill was the root cause of errors they were making. Together with the computer operations and programming departments, the bill-processing group revised the bill's format, with a resulting drop in errors. This is a good example of cross-functional cooperation.

In 1989, FPL was able to reduce errors in customer bills from 45 parts per million to 8 parts per million. Since the entire billing process is now understood as never before, the error rate will continue to improve. While the activities required to produce an accurate bill are very different from, say, manufacturing computer chips, the QIDW process to control it is nonetheless very similar. Total quality management can work in any kind of company—service or manufacturing.

At the time we introduced QIDW at FPL, we realized that our statistical quality control (SQC) knowledge and competence needed to be improved. Primarily this was because of the widespread use of more sophisticated control charts. Our goal was to train slightly over 1 percent of our employees as SQC experts. We brought in some experts from Japan and developed a six-week training course in SQC. We tried it out on a class of thirty students and, of course, made some mistakes and learned what not to do. Based on what we learned, the course was improved and, as of this writing, a total of about 230 employees have graduated from it. The graduates of the SQC course are used on a part-time basis as a resource by the rest of the company. We now have at least one employee with these skills at each major work location. Top management also took a three-day course to gain enough knowledge to be able to ask sensible questions about SQC.

With all of these QIDW systems in place and operating, it is amazing how efficiently and smoothly things run. You wonder why you did not do it sooner, but then as we learned, there is a limit to how much change an organization can handle at any one time. We probably implemented change about as fast as our people could handle it. I remember in one office a poster of Clint Eastwood pointing a forty-four at the viewer: at the bottom someone had added this caption: "Go ahead, make my day. Make one more change." Our people have a quick wit, and a sense of humor. It was about this time that I also learned they had assigned the common acronym PDCA a second meaning: namely, "Please Don't Change Anything." But, fortunately or unfortunately, improvement requires change.

# *Bright Ideas*

When I came to work for Florida Power & Light as a student engineer in 1951, one of the things I learned about in my initial orientation was the suggestion program. In time I even turned in a suggestion or two. Later I was in the position to evaluate suggestions for adoption or rejection. I understood our system and was comfortable with it. I even thought that it was a good one.

As we began to implement our Quality Improvement Program (QIP) process in 1985, it was recommended that we revise the suggestion program. The vice president of Personnel and I decided that this was not a good idea. We reasoned that the suggestion program encouraged individual initiative. What we were trying to instill was teamwork. We thought there might be a conflict between QIP teams and individual suggestions. And we both liked the old program we knew so well. How wrong can you be?

It was 1988 by the time we replaced the old FPL Suggestion Program with FPL Bright Ideas. As a result, in 1989 alone we had twice as many suggestions as we had received in the entire sixty-year history of the old program.

Why? What is so different? A comparison of the two programs shows many differences. The policies of the old program began by telling employees how much their ideas were wanted and appreciated by the company. Then followed a long list of taboo areas in which suggestions would not be accepted, such as the need for the replacement or repair of equipment (indeed anything requiring capital expenditures), legal matters, advertising, sales—the list went on and on. Over time various departments had in effect been able to opt out of the suggestion program. They just didn't want to be bothered, and anyway, they were sure they knew it all and couldn't be told what to do by anyone else in the world, certainly not by someone outside their own department. The employees inside the department knew better than to make a suggestion, so they were no threat. When a brave soul did turn in a suggestion, it seemed to disappear into a black hole. The approval process took months, even years. The average time—that's right, *average* time—for the employee to hear anything was five months.

Finally, after a suggestion went all the way to some officer of the company who would make the final decision, word would come back to the employee. Eighty percent of the time it was, "Sorry, no good, but try again." We had a suggestion program in name only. It was utterly amazing that we got any suggestions at all. But hope springs eternal, and believe it or not, about 600 suggestions were submitted in 1987. Now you may laugh at what I have just said, but I suspect that there exist many examples of programs just like our old one.

In 1989, we got not 600 but 25,000 suggestions, or an average of almost two suggestions per employee. About 50 percent of the suggestions were implemented on the spot. The others were studied further before being accepted or rejected. Over half of all employees turned in at least one suggestion in 1989. This is a vast increase, but there is still a lot of room for improvement. I have been informed that at the Milliken Company, a 1989 Baldrige Award winner, as many as eighteen suggestions per employee are turned in each year.

The single most important characteristic of a good suggestion program is a fast decision and fast response back to the employee. At Milliken they have what they call the 24/72 rule: the suggestion is acknowledged by the supervisor in 24 hours, and an answer concerning its disposition is received by the employee in 72 hours. The answer may be that the suggestion requires further study, but if this is the case, the employee receives periodic status reports. Speed seems to be a common factor in all the effective programs I have seen.

As a rule, FPL does not grant employees bonuses for quality improvement achievements. The suggestion program is a small exception. We award an employee a given number of points upon the implementation of a suggestion. If the suggestion results in significant quality improvement or cost savings, the employee can also be awarded additional points. These points are accumulated somewhat in the manner of the airlines' frequent flyer points. A rather nice catalog of items is available on which employees can "spend" their points; of course, different numbers of points are assigned to each item in the catalog. When an employee sees an item he or she likes in the catalog, the reward system encourages the employee to continue making suggestions until he or she amasses the necessary total points. Hey, it's popular.

Another difference between the old program and the new one is that the supervisor is very much involved. All suggestions go initially to the supervisor, and all status reports back to the employee are handled directly between the supervisor and employee. In the old program the suggester was anonymous, but in the new one, the suggester's name is very prominently displayed. There are several benefits to this. First, turning in a suggestion is to be encouraged and FPL wants employees to receive recognition for their ideas and effort. Second, if the evaluators/supervisors have any questions about an idea, they know whom to see. The result is a much speedier and more open process.

In addition to the catalog rewards, other types of recognition programs have also been developed, primarily locally. In one department, management takes to lunch those employees who have turned in ten or more suggestions in a current year and recognizes them for their contributions. At the corporate level, several employees are singled out for special recognition: the one who has turned in the most suggestions in a year; the one who has had the most suggestions implemented in a year; and the "suggester of the year," the employee whose suggestions have resulted in the most overall improvement.

One of the plant managers came up with the idea of attaching the suggestion form to the back of each work order. When the crew completes their paperwork for each job, they see the following question: "Do you have any suggestion for how this job might have been done better?" This innovation has been very effective because it asks the right question at the right time: when problems are still fresh in employees' minds. It also constantly keeps before the employees the idea of improving the process, reinforcing the PDCA way of thinking. This idea has proved to be so successful that it is now being adopted by the rest of the company.

The comparison of FPL's two suggestion programs is really very stark, as the data for 1987 and 1989 illustrate. In 1987, we received 636 suggestions from 2 percent of the employees. In 1989, we received over 25,000 suggestions from 53 percent of the employees. The benefits from these suggestions are enormous. In addition to the significant improvements in quality, on average almost $800 of first-year savings result from every suggestion adopted. Before Bright Ideas began, we were just fore-going the benefits of these changes—changes that really weren't very profound or difficult to enact.

We went to considerable lengths to publicize the new pro-gram and inform all employees of how they could participate in it. And we gave the supervisors a brief training course on how to encourage employees to make suggestions, how to evaluate sug-gestions properly, and on the administrative and procedural parts of the program. This was to make sure that the process didn't bog down at the supervisor level. Again, the key lies in training supervisors to respect employees and welcome their ideas, as well as setting up a very simple system to reinforce this attitude.

I also feel, however, that one reason why the new suggestion program was so amazingly successful in such a short period of time was that by the time we instituted Bright Ideas in 1988, our employees were already making a big effort to look for any im-provement that could be made. This was largely a result of their participation in team activity and QIDW. Also, by this time em-ployees had developed trust in the system and confidence that management really did mean to improve customer satisfaction. The ground had been plowed, as it were. Still we wondered why we hadn't done this sooner, because it is now so easy; it is almost like picking up fruit from the ground.

A company's suggestion program says a lot about its corpo-rate culture. If I were to pick a single quality indicator for a good corporate culture, the suggestion system would probably be it. There are a number of prerequisites for a suggestion program to be really good. Management must genuinely want suggestions and employees must know that this is so. The way they will know this is to see it in action. Especially in this instance, what you do speaks louder than what you say. There must be a system in place to approve or disapprove suggestions quickly, and to see that if they are approved, they are implemented. Employees must be attuned to thinking about improvements and customer satisfaction. Since these are all prerequisites to a good program, it follows that any company that has a large and demonstrably successful suggestion program is already doing many things right.

Yet any management can convince itself that it has quality products or a good suggestion program or anything else it wants. Even the most miserable effort can be accepted if that is the corporate culture. Unfortunately, it isn't going to get the job done. Somewhere out there is another organization of people who know where it's at, and that means everyone is working on customer satisfaction. They are your competition, and look out—here they come!

# Vendor Quality

$O$ne of FPL's major corporate quality indicators has been the number of unplanned days off-line in its nuclear power plants. In other words, it is an important indication of quality that when these plants are required and expected to be running, they are. Moreover, our customers tell us that most of all they want safe and reliable nuclear plants. Days off-line is an excellent quality indicator because it reflects performance in the quality elements of both public safety and price. It is the voice of the customer speaking to us.

Like some others, Florida Power & Light had problems with O-rings. In this case, I am talking about the three O-rings in each reactor cooling pump. The pumps will work with just one ring in operation, but because these pumps are such an important part of the plant's safety system, we would not continue to operate a nuclear plant for very long if even one O-ring wasn't working properly.

Several years ago, when we returned our very best nuclear plant to operation following a scheduled, and otherwise routine, refueling outage, one of its pumps had a leaking O-ring. To correct the problem we had to shut down the plant for an unplanned interruption. This hit our quality indicator of unplanned days off-line right in the nose. It took eight days for us to return the plant to normal operation, and of course, during these eight days we had to generate electricity by more expensive means, which impacted the price indicator.

When the problematic O-ring was removed and carefully examined, a small flaw in its manufacture was found. For as long as I can remember, at FPL we have had a reputation of buying on low initial price. We didn't worry much about quality; the goal was to obtain a low bid price, and then to negotiate an even lower price if possible. But this O-ring problem is an excellent example of how low initial price does not necessarily result in low overall cost or provide quality.

It is also a good example of why we needed a vendor quality program. Sixty percent of everything FPL uses and needs comes from outside the company. There is no way we could do a quality job of meeting customer needs and expectations without obtaining quality products and services from our vendors. It is always easier to point to someone else's problems than it is to fix your own. Maybe for this reason vendor quality programs have a relatively long history in the United States and Japan.

Back in 1984, before my first trip to Japan, we had sent twelve middle managers (who later became known as the twelve apostles) to Japan for a three-week study mission. This was a group of twelve key managers selected as a representative sample of FPL's people and departments. Carlton Hopkins, who became the godfather of the FPL Vendor Quality Improvement Program, was one of these original twelve apostles. To prepare for the trip, they had spent five weeks visiting other companies in the United States that were at the forefront of quality, and studying quality improvement theory, a serious undertaking.

We had several reasons for this study mission. The other officers and I knew we didn't understand the total quality management system at all, and we hoped that if we let managers from all areas of the company study for an extended period of time, they could transfer this knowledge to our company. They were to examine all parts of the Japanese TQM systems, take voluminous notes, and upon their return write a detailed report including their recommendations on what we should do next.

We had another, less admirable reason for sending them. At this time, top management, including myself, still felt that quality improvement was something to be delegated. We hoped we would not have to put out much effort or significantly change what we were doing. Of course, we came to learn that we were mistaken in this, but at this stage we didn't understand that.

The twelve apostles were very successful in their objective of learning about the TQM system and bringing that knowledge back to our company. Every one of those first pioneers has played a major part in our implementation of quality management at FPL. For what it is worth, their careers have also done very well. Their first and most important recommendation when they returned was that top management had to become personally involved in the quality effort. Somehow, I do think that deep down we knew this was going to be the case.

This was only the first of many study missions we sent to Japan. In time such missions came to be informally known in the company as "going to Japan for the operation." What was meant by this was that those who went on these trips came back looking at the world as if through oriental eyes. Even if this was said in somewhat rough-spirited jest, it was a pretty good metaphor. Our people did come back with different lenses through which to view their work. They saw things in a new way. They had seen the process work. They had seen that it wasn't so difficult; it wasn't anything they couldn't do themselves. They had seen people just like themselves making great progress in coping with the same problems with which they themselves were struggling. They had begun to understand how it worked. Personally they were never again quite the same, in that they had seen "the promised land" and their way of seeing and thinking had been forever changed.

I would recommend that any management considering TQM go on their own study missions. Today it's not even necessary to go to Japan; there are a number of excellent quality management systems right here in the United States. And after management goes on its study mission, they should send additional groups of employees to study what is being done. It is truly a great eye opener. All of the companies using total quality management are surprisingly open and willing to demonstrate what they are doing to improve quality. Some are even willing to show their competitors what they do.

Common to all the quality companies we visited was a comprehensive quality vendor system. It is easy to see that this makes sense. As I mentioned before, at FPL 60 percent of everything we use comes from vendors. Just pointing fingers to account for problems is easy, but implementing an effective quality vendor system is not. It is hard enough to install a quality system in one's own organization. To do something similar in an organization over which one has much less influence is harder, to say the least.

Even though we saw the need for a vendor quality program in 1985, it was not until 1987 that we rolled out our own program. When we first looked at what we buy and how we buy it, improvement seemed to be an enormous problem. Moreover, we didn't have very good data on just what our purchasing requirements were. All we understood was purchase price. To rectify this, we spent 1986 looking at ourselves and identifying just what was important to us and our customers when we make a purchase.

One of the issues we struggled with was how we could tie a

quality vendor program to our customer quality indicators. Of course, if all we wanted was low initial price, we had no problem. But by this time we knew we had to set broader requirements. In the area of price, we now felt that lifetime ownership cost was the correct indicator. To this we added the elements of quality, delivery, and safety.

Finally after much discussion, we elected to focus the vendor program on the corporate quality indicator of reliability. With this in mind, we were able to narrow down the problem and to begin to identify components of the system that had the largest impact on reliability. Initially we identified seventeen purchased products that could have a major impact on the quality indicator of reliability—things like switches, cables, meters, and transformers. We continue to add to the list. For example, in 1989 we added ten additional items. By prioritizing the sequence of the items we worked on and their vendors, we expected to have the maximum reliability improvement in the shortest time (see Figure 9.1).

We were aware, however, that the vendor improvement program would be a long-term project. Some of the expected benefits will not show up for many years, but that does not mean that such a program is not important.

At the core of the FPL vendor program is the process of working with vendors to qualify them in one of three successive levels of performance: "Quality Vendor" is the first level, "Certified Vendor" the next, and "Excellent Vendor" the highest (see Figure 9.2).

To become a Quality Vendor, a supplier's products or services must meet our requirements on quality, cost, delivery, and safety. In addition, the supplier must have a quality improvement process in place and must demonstrate that they have achieved significant improvements. Finally, they must have an audit system

### Quality Improvement Program
### For Vendors
#### Targeted Products/Services
#### 1988

1. Transmission breakers (230 KV, 500 KV, SF6)
2. Switches (substation, distribution overhead, and underground)
3. Nuclear spare parts
4. Distribution transformers (aerial and padmount)
5. Molded rubber cable accessories
6. Distribution cable
7. Distribution regulators
8. Combustion and steam turbines
9. Boilers
10. Pressurizer safety and power-operated valves
11. Nuclear fuel
12. Residential meters
13. Circuit breakers (4160 (CE) & 480V)
14. Fans (forced draft, inducted draft, gas induction)
15. Vertical pumps (cooling water and condensate)
16. Relays (substation)
17. Lamps (T&D)

#### Targeted Products/Services
#### 1989

1. Distribution surge arresters
2. Stirrup clamps
3. Insulation– installation and removal
4. Valves– fossil (boiler feedwater system)
5. Motor repair (480V-6900V)
6. Nuclear plant engineers, architects, and consulting services
7. Valves– nuclear (purge and spray)
8. Distribution breakers
9. Load management system equipment
10. Generator repair

**FIGURE 9.1 Purchased products and services targeted for vendor quality improvement.**

to certify the process and results. In 1987, we qualified our first four Quality Vendors. By the end of 1989, the list had grown to sixty-seven Quality Vendors.

To become a Certified Vendor, a company must first be an FPL Quality Vendor. In addition, they must have demonstrated the use of statistical process control (SPC) and have a process capability ($C_{pk}$) greater than 1 for each critical indicator. ($C_{pk}$ is

**FIGURE 9.2 The three levels of the vendor quality program.**

a process capability index; a $C_{pk}$ of greater than 1 means that the process can meet our specification requirements.) Finally, they must be able to document their capability and have a plan of continuous quality improvement. There are also a few administrative requirements, but what I have just described is the essence of the requirements. In 1989, we had two Certified Vendors. There will be many more. In time, there will be many Excellent Vendors as well.

Why would a vendor want to go to all this trouble and effort? There are a number of benefits, the most important being that they will have higher-quality products and services to sell not only to FPL but to all their other customers as well. Several of FPL's vendors have told me that their companies are much more competitive as a result of what they did to become a Quality Vendor for FPL. One of our first four Quality Vendors, the Nuclear Fuel Division of the Westinghouse Company, went on in 1988 to win the Malcolm Baldrige National Quality Award. John

Marous, the chairman and CEO of Westinghouse, has told me that being recognized by FPL as a Quality Vendor was a major milestone on their way to winning the Baldrige.

Additionally, both the qualifying vendor and FPL advertise the fact that the supplier company has become an FPL Quality Vendor, which helps boost employee morale.

The bottom line is that these suppliers will probably get more of FPL's business, a very important point for those who only seem to worry about the bottom line. The FPL bid evaluation process has been revised to put greater weight on quality. To this end, Quality Vendors are awarded 5 points and Certified Vendors 7 points out of a possible 100 points. One cable manufacturer has increased its share of FPL's cable purchases from 16 percent to 36 percent in the two years since they became a Quality Vendor.

So what! What does all this mean to FPL's customers? Well, for example, our data on long-duration electrical outages showed us that a principal cause of these outages was direct-buried, underground electrical cable. By looking into the causes of these cable failures, we learned that manufacturing irregularities in the thickness of the cable and insulation were the principal culprits.

We began to work with the manufacturers of this type of cable to improve the statistical quality control of their operations. The result has been a great reduction in the variability of the insulation of the cable we purchase, and a much longer cable life. This will improve the service reliability to FPL customers, which is what we set out to do in the first place.

In addition to higher-quality products, we have also benefited from improvements in other areas of vendor performance, such as delivery. For example, late delivery by vendors to FPL was reduced from 88 percent in 1987 to 27 percent at year end 1989. This improvement enables FPL to better meet its scheduled commitments to its customers. Within these numbers on late performance, large differences still exist between vendors, but those who are not performing well are beginning to stick out like a sore thumb. You might say that their days are numbered.

One day as I thought about the credit we give quality vendors, I asked Carlton Hopkins how much more we were paying for higher-quality products. He laughed and said, "Not very much." He said that the quality vendors have turned out to be the most competitive in price. After thinking for a moment, I realized I should have known that. As a result of their quality improvement efforts, FPL's vendors have also become more efficient, just as FPL has.

# *Education and Training*

$A$t the end of the Deming examination, when I was asked what three things I would advise another CEO who wanted to install total quality management, the second thing I mentioned was that they should be prepared to make a major commitment to education and training. To progress from a traditionally managed company to one using TQM, everyone must acquire new knowledge. But what is more important, people must be educated in a new and different way of doing things—a new way of working. They need to become practitioners of TQM. All of this takes time, effort, and on-the-job practice.

The benefits of TQM are great, but of course there is some expense involved, mainly in this area of education and training. In FPL's case, it was a rather modest amount; the total Quality Improvement Program (QIP) training budget has never equaled even 1 percent of the operations and maintenance budget. In fact, the most we spent on QIP training in one year was $6 million. Nonetheless, it was a considerable increase for us, although I suspect that we should have done even more training than we did.

During the entire postwar period our training expenses were small and had grown slowly. Most of our efforts had gone into skills training—mainly apprentice training and safety procedures training. In the 1950s we began to add a series of after-hours minicourses to help our employees keep their job-related knowledge up-to-date. Then in the 1970s, with the introduction of a new management team, we began to become more active in education. About a hundred of our managers and officers were sent to short courses offered at university business schools, and we brought in outside experts to teach us various new management practices. That is about where we were at the beginning of the 1980s.

I have mentioned several times the trip I took with several other officers to Japan in 1984 to study TQM—the trip that brought us to Kansai Electric in Osaka and was our big eye opener. This was not, however, the first excursion from FPL. As we began to get more serious about quality improvement in the early 1980s, we realized that education and training were going to be key to our success. When we were developing our early training courses we felt that there was a good deal we could learn from Japanese companies. Therefore, in 1983, we sent two of our employees, Kent Sterett and Judy Divita, to Japan to observe quality management in operation. Kent later became the director of the Quality Improvement Department and Judy was the manager of our Training Department. These are the two key staff jobs in the implementation of TQM.

Kent is about 6'4" tall, which makes him stand out in Japan. Judy is about 5'3" tall, and in addition to being a manager at FPL, she was also expecting her first child at that time. I think that the two of them must have made quite an impression at the companies they visited.

At some point, I suppose I should confess that in the beginning I was not a supporter of QIP. In fact, I was against it. I had heard about Japanese quality circles and how they were not very successful in America. Moreover, our chairman at that time had a history of trying out every new management scheme that came along. In the beginning I thought QIP was just another "flavor of the month" idea he had heard about somewhere. In fact, I thought that on this one he was a little behind the times. Even so, by 1984 I had to admit that some of our teams were undoubtedly getting good results, and the team members certainly seemed enthusiastic about what they were doing. So I guess you could say that I was beginning to have doubts about my doubts.

At that point in time we were trying to tightly control costs, partly by using zero-based budgets. (I might add that we were not having much success in our cost-control efforts. In fact, we seemed to have a rate case pending before the Public Service Commission every year.) As a part of each year's budget we thoroughly reviewed the proposed training plans and expenses. In 1982 and 1983, we had been allocating more and more time and money to QIP team leader and facilitator training, and even top managers had attended a three-day orientation course on QIP. Even though we were making a dramatic increase in training budgets, I noticed that we ran through the budget each year by about July and were asked to make an additional allocation for QIP training.

Historically, we had to work very hard to meet our training plan, but this was not true of QIP. Something very different was going on. For example, in 1983 we planned to train a total of 2,693 employees; we actually trained 2,622. However, inside these numbers lies a different story: we had planned to train 340 in QIP and actually trained 714, whereas in all the other more traditional areas we had planned training for 2,282 and only achieved 1,976. In 1984, the trend became more pronounced: we had planned to train 144 additional team leaders and actually trained 749. Our employees were telling us something, and we were beginning to hear. By this time the officers of the company, including myself, had taken three courses on quality improvement. We had learned a lot. The most important lesson was that the process worked and produced positive results. This was why the training was so popular with our employees—it was useful to them.

We have always preferred at FPL to conduct training in house. The instructors are not always as skilled as outsiders, but because they understand the company, they have greater credibility. We elected to continue this practice with our QIP training.

Our Training Department develops and tests new courses as needed, and then trains a group of line managers who in turn become the training instructors for the rest of the company. In 1982, we developed our first two QIP training courses: one in team leader training and one in facilitator training. In 1984, we added leadership for managers I and II and supervisor and foreman awareness courses. In 1985, as things really got going, we added supervising for quality and leadership for managers III, all the while continuing to accelerate the existing team programs. That year we trained 1,106 new team leaders. By 1989 we had developed thirteen of our own QIP training courses at FPL, and FPL's employees had taken more than 40,000 formal training courses, not counting on-the-job training. This gives some idea of what I mean by commitment to education and training.

Not only did we develop our training courses, we have also had to update them from time to time. American training consultants had helped us put together our first team leader and facilitator courses. These courses served their purpose for a while, but they had been developed by the company using what we had learned in America. By 1986, we were learning many new lessons with the help of our Japanese counselors. We realized that what the teams were actually doing in the field was more advanced than what we were teaching in the classroom. For example, our teams were using all seven of the basic problem-solving tools, even though our initial training taught only three of them. By 1986 we were including training in all seven and were updating the team case study examples used in these courses. In 1989 we had to update these courses again.

Conversely, as we began to train our supervisors and managers more completely, we found that we could drop some of the less intense orientation programs for managers.

From the start, our Japanese counselors took a keen interest in education and training—no doubt because it is so important to TQM, but perhaps also because they were themselves university professors. They kept pushing us to improve training and to be able to show with data that knowledge was in fact being transferred to the students. We constantly had to use the plan-do-check-act cycle on our training efforts, testing and surveying our students over and over. But the effort paid off: when we looked at the before and after test scores, we could see the improvement in our teaching abilities. Today the employees who act as instructors are seasoned practitioners who have learned by doing, not just by reading books. They know what they are talking about and it shows.

In 1987, we introduced a rather advanced course on statistical quality control. We knew that we had made some mistakes our first time through the course, and we planned to improve it, but that wasn't good enough for Dr. Asaka, who was very dissatisfied when he looked over the results of our first SQC class. He suggested we get Dr. Kenji Kurogane to help us with SQC. In addition to being a well-known expert in SQC, Dr. Kurogane is an expert on fisheries and fishing, and a counselor to one of the Japanese breweries. In due time Dr. Kurogane came to FPL. He was somewhat different from our other Japanese counselors and acquaintances. For one thing, he is very jolly and somewhat overweight—a sort of Japanese Santa Claus. I thought that anyone who looks so cheery, fishes, and drinks beer has to be okay!

I remember very well sitting through the first of Dr. Kurogane's classes. We had selected about twenty of our best SQC practitioners to make presentations on their best SQC applications. Our people were rather proud of their work, as was I, but pride goeth before a fall. Dr. Kurogane pointed out the weak points in each presentation, a somewhat humbling experience. But he was so good-natured about it that no one's feelings were hurt.

By this time we were going through many humbling experiences. We were learning something new every day, but what we kept learning over and over was that we still had a lot to learn. IBM has a motto, "There is no saturation to education." How true it is! Quality improvement is a never-ending journey, and so is education. A case in point is the training budget at Motorola (a 1988 Malcolm Baldrige Award winner), which has gone from $7 million a year to $120 million—and they find that these are some of the best dollars they spend.

One of the auxiliary benefits of employee training is that it produces higher morale. When a company makes an effort to improve its employees, they receive a very strong, positive message of appreciation and respect.

Another side benefit of our QIP activities and education was that word got back to the college campuses. Our recruiters noted that FPL's reputation had become so good that we were attracting a higher quality of new employee than they could ever remember.

People at all levels in the company were learning, but management was learning the most of all. Top management has to be involved with TQC training from the start, although team training should follow soon after.

I recall one of our early 1986 policy deployment presentations very well. We sent minutes of the presentation to our counselors in Japan for their feedback. Now, in an hour-and-a-half presentation I had cut off the speaker about thirty times to ask questions. In their own tactful way, each of our counselors got word back to me that I should please shut up and listen, make notes, and ask my questions at the end of the presentation if necessary, but let the poor speaker have a chance.

The most meaningful lesson in all my education was just that: shut up and listen. Listen to your customers and what they are saying. Listen to your employees and let them help you identify and solve the company's problems. Give your people a chance to show how good they can be. Invest in them with education and training, and then listen to them. To say it another way, stop falling over your own ego and begin to have more respect for people. Not only I, but every one of our managers ultimately had to learn this lesson, and many American managers need to do the same. This was probably the most important thing we learned from our Japanese counselors. As they put it, and as I have stressed in so many other contexts, the fourth principle of TQM is respect for people.

# *Results*

*I*n one of his clinics, Dr. Yoshio Kondo (another of our counselors) talked about the importance of the scoreboard. He asked us to think about a basketball game between two evenly matched teams. The lead keeps changing as first one, then the other team sinks a basket. As the game progresses and the clock becomes a factor, time-outs are taken for the teams and coaches to plot strategy. And finally as the game draws to an end, it builds to a climax of excitement for the fans and players. "Now," said Dr. Kondo, "imagine the same game without a scoreboard."

Sometimes we had difficulty understanding what our counselors were trying to teach us, but this time Dr. Kondo's point was crystal clear. There would be no build-up of excitement and probably little interest in such a game because no one would know who was leading, how much time was left, or even who won. It is the difference between the NBA championship and a practice session.

Setting goals for ourselves and striving to achieve them brings us to do our very best. And it's exciting and fun as the contest nears its finish.

In total quality management the results serve as the quality improvement scoreboard; therefore, results need to be made visible to everyone who is making a contribution to the effort, in other words, to just about everyone in the company. These results are what keep people going when the trials and tribulations come along. There were times in the early days of FPL's quality improvement program when an anecdote of one team's success kept us going. We would share each success with one another to prove to ourselves that we could do it, and that it was worth doing.

As the number of teams grew from 200 in 1983 to 700 in 1984, the number of good stories grew apace. We still had our annoyances and our disappointments—to a lesser extent, this is still true today. (I guess that's just human nature.) But the bad news became easier and easier to counter as the amount of good news increased. As time went on, of course, we were overwhelmed with such anecdotes and we developed greater sophistication and higher expectations and standards for ourselves. But it is still the results, big and small, that we can see and measure and share with each other that keep us going.

Despite a good beginning with our teams, it was not until 1985, when we began to implement policy management and the entire TQM system, that we could see and measure major results at the corporate level. That was when we began to see significant and consistent improvement on FPL's corporate quality improvement objectives. That was when we began to have a better understanding of what our customers wanted and how we went about fulfilling those wants.

Because we really did not have a corporate scoreboard before that time, a great deal of effort went into deciding just what results were the correct ones to measure. We did a pretty good job of selecting those quality indicators the first time around. About half of those first indicators are still being used five years later, including things like the number of complaints to the Florida Public

Service Commission per thousand customers; the average number of minutes per year customers are without electricity; and, most important of all the indicators, the results of customer satisfaction surveys.

Of course we made mistakes. In some cases, we set out to measure activity instead of quality: for example, the number of people trained in QIP or the number of teams in operation. In time we learned that these were not the correct measurements for quality. These data may be useful, but they should not be mislabeled as indicators of quality. Quality indicators measure those things that show improvement in satisfying the customer.

One of our worst errors in this regard was deciding to include the number of team solutions per year as a quality indicator. We set, as a minimum, at least one problem solution or improvement action memo (IAM) per year per team. From our visits to Japan we knew that quality circles there typically produced a solution in three or four months, so we thought our teams should be able to come up with at least one IAM in a year's time. Well, that's just what we got—activity, not quality.

We learned later that as year-end approached, attention became focused on the number of IAMs outstanding. Our managers told the teams to finish up, no matter how they did it. Some teams even took an insignificant little problem that had already been solved, retrofitted it to the QI story, and called it an IAM.

This greatly damaged the credibility of our entire program, and it took us a long time to live it down. In fact, about a year later when we surveyed employees on how QIP was going, we could still see traces of the problem we had caused.

In addition to selecting the right kinds of results as quality indicators, it is very important that both corporate and departmental results be made visible to all employees. At Florida Power & Light, this is accomplished in many ways. Quality improvement team story boards are hung on the walls throughout the company. Anyone who passes by them can stop and see what a team did and the results of its efforts. Results of the better team solutions are also communicated by means of both the printed and taped house organs and the expos we hold twice a year so that teams can tell their QI stories.

Quality in Daily Work (QIDW) control charts are also displayed on the walls throughout the company. Passersby can see the important things the department is trying to control and how they are doing. Bright Idea suggestions are publicized from time to time as well.

But the most important results of all are the ones associated with customer satisfaction. Each department has its own set of indicators in support of corporate goals. And, as I have already mentioned, we developed a considerable number of corporate quality indicators to measure the results of our policy management objectives.

Again, this series of quality indicators is the company equivalent of the game scoreboard. Since everyone needs to know how they and the company are doing over time and on a current basis, data on progress toward the corporate indicators are distributed monthly to a large number of managers, who are asked to share the information with their employees. At the end of each year, a report on our progress as a company toward corporate quality goals is sent to all employees. To underscore its importance, this report is mailed to each employee's home.

The results on these corporate quality indicators are broken down into their components. For example, the companywide result on customers' average minutes per year without electricity is subdivided to show the impact of each of our five regional divisions, and then further broken down into the portion represented by each of the twenty districts. These subdivisions are then examined by cause (lightning, trees, vehicles, etc.). Each of these is also looked at from the point of view of frequency and duration of outages. All these results are shared with all of the departmental employees who are making a contribution toward their improvement.

As the results begin to show progress toward quality improvement, people can see that the system works. They start to think that their effort is worthwhile. Although it is undoubtedly beneficial to foster this outlook, it is not the only reason you need to measure how you are doing.

The principal reason for measuring results is for the purpose of analysis—the "check" part of PDCA, if you will. Each operational unit of the company plans a number of projects to improve how we serve the customer. And as the projects are implemented, questions must be asked: How did the projects turn out? Were the predicted results achieved? Was more or less improvement realized? Why? The results are analyzed to see what we can learn to improve the process for the next PDCA cycle. The results of team improvement actions, QIDW control systems, and suggestions are all analyzed in this manner. Every action is put through the check cycle for verification and learning purposes.

To determine the divisional and total corporate results, the operational units' results are combined on a weighted basis. This is done as often as necessary—in some cases this means daily or weekly, but at the corporate level, monthly is generally good enough. A periodic review of the results is conducted by management so that mid-course countermeasures can be taken to keep the company on track. First the results are reviewed at the district level, and then at the division level. Ultimately, these local results are combined with the overall corporate results, which are then reviewed to be sure we'll meet our targets. If things are not working out as well as expected, additional projects may have to be added to the plan. Resources may need to be taken from some other area where the results are better than expected so as to stay within the budget. Because of these intermediate check steps, FPL has been able to meet a very high percentage of its goals and objectives.

In 1985 and 1986 we were still learning how to focus our quality improvement efforts on those things that would produce the greatest customer satisfaction. By 1987, we had identified eight priority functions that were really important as communicated to us by the voice of the customer (see Figure 11.1). We then selected the appropriate quality indicator, or result, that would help us monitor our progress in each of these priority areas.

| LEGEND: ⊙ High ○ Medium △ Low     COMPANY GOALS<br><br>PRIORITY AREAS | 1. Improve customer satisfaction with sales and service quality | 2. Strengthen effectiveness in nuclear plant operation and regulatory performance | 3. Improve utilization of resources to stabilize costs |
|---|---|---|---|
| SALES & SERVICE QUALITY — Reduce customer dissatisfaction | ⊙ | | △ |
| Increase customer satisfaction | ⊙ | | △ |
| Reduce service unavailability | ⊙ | | ○ |
| RELIABILITY — Reduce transmission forced outages | ⊙ | △ | ○ |
| Increase nuclear availability | ○ | ⊙ | ⊙ |
| Reduce fossil forced outages | ⊙ | | ⊙ |
| SAFETY — Improve nuclear safety | | ⊙ | ○ |
| Improve employee safety | | | ○ |

**FIGURE 11.1  Eight priority areas for improvement, based on customer needs.**

The quality indicator for reducing customer dissatisfaction, the first priority area listed, is the number of complaints to the Florida Public Service Commission (PSC) per thousand FPL customers (see Figure 11.2). When we began to measure complaints to the PSC in 1985, Florida Power & Light was in a virtual tie for worst with the most complaints of any Florida utility. Figure 11.2 shows the dramatic reduction we achieved in the number of these complaints. Overall the complaints have dropped from 0.9 per 1,000 customers in 1984 to 0.3 at the end of 1988 to 0.23 at the end of 1989; the 1992 goal is 0.16. From 1984 to 1989, FPL has gone from one of the worst utilities to one of the best in the state of Florida in terms of number of customer complaints.

In the past, we had all sorts of excuses for why we were so bad. We used to say, for example, that our customers were more obstreperous than those of the other utilities. It is obvious that

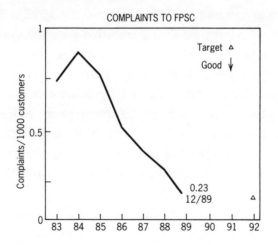

**FIGURE 11.2  The quality indicator for reducing customer dissatisfaction—number of complaints to the Florida Public Service Commission.**

these were nothing more than rationalizations for poor management.

Bing Crosby used to sing that you have to "accentuate the positive" as well as "eliminate the negative." Actions you take to delight the customer are different from those needed to reduce dissatisfaction. At FPL we have had more difficulty with delighting, the second priority item listed in Figure 11.1. One way we have tried to delight is to make sure that every customer contact with the people of FPL is pleasant and courteous. One way we measure this is by monitoring interactions and recording when they are not up to standard. The percentage of times when improvement is needed in the caring and concern for the customer dropped from 13 percent to 3.5 percent by the end of 1988. The 1992 target is 2 percent.

Great progress has also been made on the goal to reduce service unavailability (the third priority item), which has dropped from an average of 75 minutes per year per customer in 1983 to 47 minutes at the end of 1989. The goal for 1992 is 30 minutes (see Figure 11.3). Figure 11.3 shows that we apparently had perverse results in 1986. As we were improving our ability to measure results, we found that in prior years we had undercounted the number of customers affected by some electricity outages. The data were corrected for subsequent years, but not for the historic part of the graph. The lesson in this experience was that results are not always what one expects, and that the measurement system must be accurate—and also that one has to learn from mistakes and go on.

One quality indicator in the priority area of reliability is the number of transmission line forced outages. Early in 1989, we found we were not meeting this goal. If we had done nothing more at that time, we would not have met our year-end target,

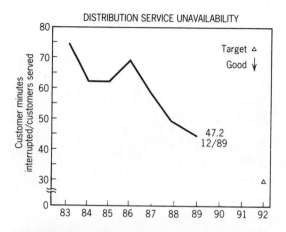

**FIGURE 11.3 The results on reducing service unavailability.**

but we took additional midyear countermeasures and came in a little better than planned (see Figure 11.4).

Another quality indicator for reliability is nuclear unplanned days off-line (see Figure 11.5). This one has been up and down at FPL but is generally heading in the right direction.

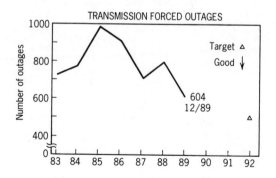

**FIGURE 11.4 An indicator for reliability—number of forced outages of transmission lines.**

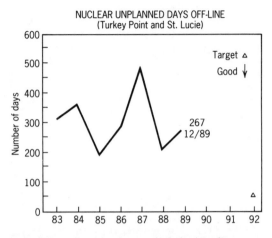

**FIGURE 11.5   Another reliability indicator—unplanned days nuclear plants are off-line.**

The final corporate indicator for reliability is fossil forced outage rate, which has shown an amazing improvement (see Figure 11.6). The measurement used for this indicator is the percentage of time the fossil-fueled plants are not available to make electric-

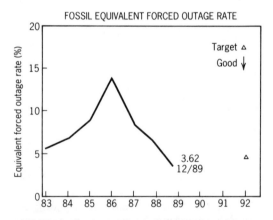

**FIGURE 11.6   A third quality indicator for reliability—percentage of time fossil-fueled plants are unavailable.**

ity. In the early 1980s we were spending more and more money on maintenance for these plants, with poorer and poorer results. With the start of policy management, the forced outage rate has plunged: by the end of 1988 it had reversed its trend and dropped to 7 percent. This indicator has continued to improve, and in 1990 it went below 3 percent—the best in America.

One result that really caught my eye when I made my second trip to Kansai Power Company in 1985 was the dramatic reduction they had achieved in the occurrence of automatic trips (shutdowns) at their nuclear power plants. This statistic is our quality indicator for nuclear safety, another of our priority items. Kansai had been in about the same position as FPL in 1981 but had subsequently passed us by and left us far behind. The last time I checked they were at zero. We haven't caught up to them yet, but we are gaining ground (see Figure 11.7).

Earlier in my life with FPL, I was in charge of the construc-

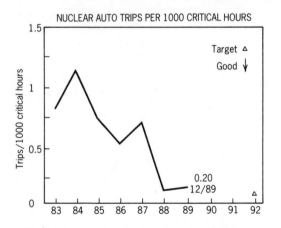

**FIGURE 11.7  Results for the quality element of nuclear safety are indicated by the occurrence of nuclear plant automatic shutdowns, or trips.**

tion and operation of electric power lines. One of my greatest worries during that time was that someone working for me would have a serious accident, so I have always had a keen interest in employee safety. Of all the company's major quality indicators, the only one that addresses the internal customer is employee safety.

The quality indicator in this priority area is lost-time injuries per 100 employees. In the past when management instituted a big safety campaign things would generally improve; then when management began to work on some other problem things would get worse again. Using QIP, lost-time accidents have dropped from 1.2 per 100 employees in 1986 to 0.4 in 1989 (see Figure 11.8). That represents a reduction of over 100 lost-time accidents per year—something to be proud of, indeed.

Another of FPL's major goals is to maintain stability in the price of electricity, through improvements in the major priority areas of sales and service, reliability, and safety. Our goal has been to keep the price of electricity below the rate of the Consumer's

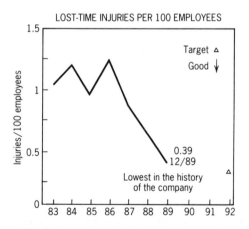

**FIGURE 11.8 Employee safety, a key priority area, shows significant results.**

Price Index. That would mean that in constant dollars there is no increase in price. From the mid-1970s to 1985 we never came close to doing that. Since 1985, with QIP, we have done very well. In nominal dollars the price of electricity by 1989 was down 10 percent (see Figure 11.9). In constant dollars the price was down 30 percent. Moreover, for the years 1985 through 1989, FPL has earned the full amount allowed by the Florida Public Service Commission and provided a refund to customers to boot. All of our gains in efficiency have added up, and they show up at the bottom line.

I am often asked how much money FPL spent on QIP. In truth I don't know, but I do know that it's much, much less than the enormous savings QIP has provided.

For comparison's sake, consider the following. In 1986, when we had a 15 percent forced outage rate at our fossil fuel power plants, we had to have a 20 percent reserve margin in generating capacity. Because of the lower forced outage rate we have achieved

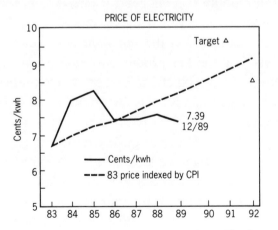

**FIGURE 11.9 Improvements in all the priority areas add up—and keep the price of electricity down.**

at our fossil power plants, we can now meet our reliability standard with only a 15 percent reserve margin in generating capacity. This lower reserve margin means that we can have the same
reliability of electric supply with one less power plant to build
and pay for. A back-of-the-envelope estimate of what the improvement in this one quality indicator saves our customers is
$400 million a year. In comparison, the most we have ever spent
on QIP training in any year is $6 million. And this is just one of
the savings and improvements in customer service that has resulted from our implementation of TQM.

I don't know how to answer the question, "What does quality
cost?" The better question is, "How much does good quality save?"
During the implementation stage of quality improvement at FPL,
we focused on quality and customer satisfaction. We did not address productivity, efficiency, or cost control. This was by design.
Throughout the postwar period FPL had pushed for productivity
and cost control, but in the early 1980s we were not getting
much of either. For the ten years from 1975 through 1984, we
had to ask the utility commission for one rate increase after another. Now we were trying a totally different approach: quality
improvement. Because we did not want our employees to think
that QIP was just another productivity improvement scheme in
disguise, we did not talk about cost at all. Of course, we never
lost sight of the fact that price is important to our customers, and
earnings to our investors, but the best way to satisfy both turned
out to be the indirect way of quality improvement. That is exactly what we saw when we looked at the Deming Prize-winning
companies in Japan. If you are a "bottom line" sort of person,
there should be a real lesson here for you.

One study I recall included the following data. In Japan all of
the Deming winners have survived. Moreover, for the period 1965
to 1985 the Deming winners have had increases in sales and profits of 14 percent. By comparison, other Japanese companies

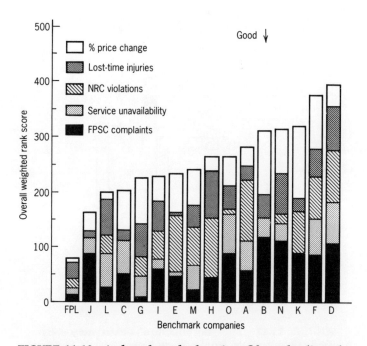

**FIGURE 11.10   As benchmarked against fifteen leading electric utilities, FPL's 1992 targets for key quality indicators will put it in the lead.**

averaged 12 percent. For the same period, American companies averaged 8 percent.

One way or another, financial analysts and Wall Street need to appreciate this lesson. I am hopeful that the financial results of the companies that have won the Malcolm Baldrige Award will begin to stand out from other companies, thereby spreading the word to more and more people throughout corporate America.

All of our counselors kept pressing us with the questions, "How will you know when you are the best-managed electric utility company? How will you measure it?" At FPL we will learn from anyone, and we will borrow a good idea from anyone. Here we took a page from our friends at Xerox and did a little benchmarking. In 1988 one of our managers, Bob Young, worked out the

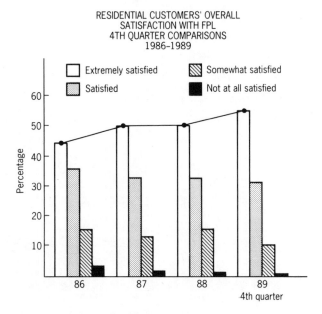

RESIDENTIAL CUSTOMERS' OVERALL
SATISFACTION WITH FPL
4TH QUARTER COMPARISONS
1986–1989

**FIGURE 11.11 The "bottom line"—extremely satisfied customers up from 45% to 55%.**

method. First, we selected fifteen other leading electric utilities with which to compare ourselves, chosen on the basis of size, reputation, and location. Next we tried to obtain data on their functions, data that would be comparable to our own quality indicators. We were successful in five areas: change in price, lost-time injuries, Nuclear Regulatory Commission (NRC) violations, service unavailability, and Public Service Commission (PSC) complaints. Then, going back to the start of policy management at FPL in 1985, we benchmarked ourselves against these fifteen utilities.

In 1985 we didn't stack up so well; we were thirteenth out of the sixteen. By 1988, we had improved to third place, and in 1989 we moved to second. If FPL achieves its 1992 goals it will be in first place (see Figure 11.10). It may well be there sooner.

AUTHOR PHOTO

A few of the key players: (l–r) Hajime Makabe, Kent Sterett, Tetsuichi Asaka, No-riko Hosoyamada, and the author.

Dr. Tetsuichi Asaka, lead counselor to FPL.

Presentation by FPL's General Office during the Deming exam.

FPL employees responding to questions during the Schedule B phase of the Deming exam.

Support room in operation during the Schedule A exam.

Multitudes of files needed to be transported through the office in milk crates during the preparation for the Deming exam and during the exam itself.

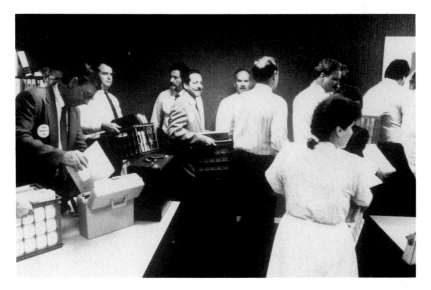

Deming examiners taking notes during a presentation. (l–r: Mr. Soma, Dr. Y. Washio, Mr. Y. Tsuda, Dr. H. Kume, Dr. I. Kusaba, Dr. M. Imaizomi.)

Submitting information to examiner Dr. Y. Akao during Schedule B.

The author fielding questions during the Schedule A examination.

FPL's Deming Prize coordinator Wayne Brunetti showing quality improvement trends.

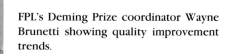

Vendor QIP manager Carlton Hopkins discussing FPL's vendor program with Dr. Kusaba, the chief examiner.

Dr. Hitoshi Kume during a lighter moment in the exam.

Top officers from Kansai Electric and FPL and FPL's counselors with commemorative banner.

The author accepts the Deming Prize on behalf of FPL; Tokyo 1989.

1989 Deming Prize winners (author seated 3rd from right).

1989年度デミング賞授賞式

Dr. W. Edwards Deming (l) and the author.

President Reagan announcing the creation of the Malcolm Baldrige National Quality Award (in the White House), 1987.

I told our counselors that when this happens we can say we have reached our vision of being the best-managed utility.

Can this also be measured with the more familiar ways used to survey customer satisfaction? It sure can. From 1986 until 1989 the percentage of FPL customers who say they are extremely satisfied with FPL has gone from 45 percent to 55 percent (see Figure 11.11). That is the real bottom line.

To sum up, FPL's quality indicators measure those things our customers say are important to them. We listen to the voice of the customer. Then we work to do a better and better job of meeting their needs and expectations. That is what policy management and the quality improvement process are all about. That is the scoreboard, and when you are winning it is exciting and fun—and it is reflected in the bottom line.

# *Recognition*

$A$s I have said before, we will go anywhere if we think we can learn something about quality improvement. On one such trip I heard Dr. Tom Malone, the president of Milliken Company, use another sports analogy to make a point about recognition. He instructed his audience to visualize the Super Bowl, and then told us to imagine the game without any cheering fans in the stadium and the impact this would have on the players. Would the players put out as much effort? Probably not. We all need cheering fans if we are truly going to excel.

We built recognition into our quality process from the start. When a team completed its improvement action memo (IAM) and quality improvement (QI) story, they made a presentation to their lead team. Those IAMs that were deemed to be very good were selected for presentation to the next level of lead team. Finally, twice a year, the fourteen best teams in the company were chosen to make presentations to the top officers of the company. Following this, the team members together with their managers and spouses attended a big dinner to celebrate the teams' accomplishments.

We had created a hierarchy of recognition and were happy with it. The twenty-eight teams honored in a year were also happy with it. What we found out later was that most of the other teams, who had also done very good work, were feeling like losers.

We realized that we had to find a better way to recognize the teams for their efforts. This materialized in the form of a Quality Improvement Program (QIP) expo held by each department or division twice a year for all their teams who have recently completed an IAM. The team members' families are invited to attend, and typically about a hundred different teams will get a chance to tell their QI stories to their managers, fellow employees, and families. It is an all-day, fun affair; everyone is equal and every team is a winner. Only later do we select teams with superior quality improvement stories for corporate recognition. As mentioned previously, from the top twenty-eight teams we also select the best four to travel around the United States and to Japan as representatives of the company.

Another way in which Florida Power & Light recognizes the team members is by hanging their pictures, along with their QI stories, on the walls throughout the company.

One thing FPL has not done is pay people directly for quality improvement; for example, teams do not receive pay for a good problem solution. However, FPL's bonus, promotion, and other human resource systems are geared to recognize QIP performance. When someone is selected for promotion in management, you may be sure that their success in leading and coaching their people and in other QIP activities was a major consideration.

With QIP we expect our employees to shine and to do great things. They need and deserve a cheering audience to appreciate what they do, but the people they want most in the audience may not be the ones you would expect. Through our 1987 employee survey on QIP, which included a number of questions about the recognition process, our employees told us that the most meaningful form of recognition was seeing their ideas implemented and producing results. Next in importance was having their supervisors and fellow workers know who did it and appreciate their accomplishments.

As time has gone by we have emphasized timely local recognition more and more. Recognition is best when it is for real accomplishment and when it comes from those persons who mean the most to us. Of course, having the powers-that-be appreciate a good job is also nice, but it is not the most important thing and it is no substitute for a good measure of on-the-spot recognition and pats on the back by local management.

Our counselors always found at least two things in each presentation to praise before they offered any criticism. Admittedly, there were times when they had to strain to locate anything worth praising, and this did not escape the notice of our employees: in an employee skit staged at a retirement party, the person playing the part of a counselor praised the ink and paper on which a report had been written. As I've said before, our people never lost their sense of humor.

The period immediately following the reviews of a department's policy deployment results was a good time for upper management to recognize real progress being made by whole departments. Our people knew they were the ones who were getting the results. They were making good things happen, they knew how they had done it, and they wanted management to know it also. As time went on, the other officers and I really began to appreciate what people were making happen, and it became a genuine joy to go around the company and recognize all the good work. When you get to this point, it is a little hard not to get excited about quality.

Recognition from outside the company can also have a tremendous impact on morale. We have always encouraged our people to participate in industry groups; a number of them attend meetings and conventions. I began to hear from our employees that they had been the center of attention when the subject of quality improvement came up. And I've seen at first hand FPL employees make a presentation at a conference and then be surrounded by members of the audience as if they were rock stars. When employees have this kind of experience they feel so good about it that upon their return to the company they have to stop people in the halls to tell them about it.

Stories began to appear in magazines and newspapers about FPL's quality improvement efforts. In the late 1970s, before QIP, the company was criticized so much by the local newspapers and by its customers that many employees would not even admit in public that they worked for FPL. By 1987 they took a new pride in the company and were proud to say so. The quality improvement program was largely responsible for this turnaround.

The final form of recognition FPL has received is the Deming Prize itself. We went into QIP to achieve customer satisfaction. We went for the Deming Prize to accelerate our progress in implementing QIP. Nonetheless, once you have put forth the kind of effort we did, it is gratifying to win the prize and get the recognition that goes with it. We all like to hear the cheering in the stands.

# The Deming Prize Preparation, Part 1

*I* am frequently asked why Florida Power & Light chose to go for the Deming Prize—an understandable question since apparently no company outside Japan had ever considered the idea, or at least had never pursued it.

In our visits to prize-winning Japanese companies it became clear to us that they were strong, healthy organizations with good products, strong customer relations, and excellent profitability over many years. Something about the process of successfully challenging for the prize seemed to create corporate strength. Some companies we visited told us they had done everything as if they were going to challenge but had decided not to. They felt they had gotten the same benefits without all the pain. We just did not see it that way. The prize-winning companies had a sparkle and their employees a fire in their eyes that the more laid-back ones lacked. The difference was obvious almost the minute we drove through the main gate.

In essence, then, the answer is that we wanted that extra impetus in implementing our quality system that comes from the challenge and preparation for the examination. The recognition that comes to the company from the prize itself is nice, but strictly secondary. We wanted FPL to be the best and we felt that the way to get there was to challenge for the Deming Prize.

Even when we made our trip to Japan in 1984, we knew something about the Deming Prize. We were aware that Kansai Electric Power Company had just won it that year. What we did not know or appreciate was just how monumental that accomplishment was.

On the second night of that first Japanese trip, we had a formal dinner in Tokyo with the people from the Union of Japanese Scientists and Engineers (JUSE). The following day we visited JUSE to hear a presentation on Japanese quality management and the role of JUSE in the Deming Prize process. In some material we were given we noticed mention of an overseas category for the Deming Application Prize. We asked about it and were told that there wasn't much to say yet since no one had ever won or even applied for the overseas prize. Thus, an idea was born.

We were aware that TQM included a process called policy management, or policy deployment; in fact, we had made a small start toward policy deployment at FPL in 1984. One of the explicit objectives of our trip was to learn more about policy deployment as we traveled around Japan. We visited two prize-winning companies in the Tokyo area and two more in Osaka. At each company we asked about policy deployment. They explained, and we listened, but we did not understand. The last of the companies we visited was Kansai Electric in Osaka. Their presentation included some very impressive results achieved through the policy deployment process, results that were understandable to us because they applied to some of the same areas with which we were struggling. We decided to return to Kansai on another trip and spend more time and effort to learn how policy deployment worked.

On each of our following trips to Japan it was our custom to visit JUSE. At all times they were very helpful to us in every way. On one trip at the end of 1985, we asked JUSE if a company like FPL could apply for the overseas Deming Prize. They requested some time to think about their answer.

On that 1985 trip, our itinerary ended as usual at the Kansai Power Company in Osaka. While we were there we met for the first time some of our new counselors: Drs. Yoshio Kondo, Hajime Makabe, and Noriaki Kano. Later, in June of 1986, we met Dr. Tetsuichi Asaka. These four men were our counselors throughout the implementation of QIP, with Dr. Asaka as the lead counselor. They were all university professors who had assisted many companies in Japan with TQM. Each of them had an established reputation and, except for Dr. Kano who was younger, they were also relatively senior in age.

The counselors were very concerned in the beginning about FPL's dedication to improving quality. They had already seen many American companies dabble with the installation of TQC, but most faltered and quit somewhere along the way. They did not want to waste their time on that kind of effort. It took us more than a year to convince them that we were absolutely serious. Dr. Kano will always be a favorite of mine because he was the first to commit to us.

The four of them and the six top officers of our company were organized as the steering committee for QIP. The role of the committee, which met in Tokyo semiannually, was to plan and direct the promotion and implementation of our quality improvement efforts.

It became my practice to meet privately with Dr. Asaka after our steering committee meetings to discuss confidential matters. After the second steering committee meeting in 1986, I told Dr. Asaka that it was my desire to challenge for the Deming Application Prize in 1989. He replied that a Japanese company of our size and at our current level of TQC would need at least three years, even if they worked very hard. Given the problems of distance, language, and culture, where FPL was concerned, it would be very, very difficult for us to do. But he did not say no, and at least he knew almost from the start that we were determined to go as far as our efforts and talents would take us.

By this time we had heard the stories about how long and hard the employees of companies worked as the time of the exam approached—the stories of managers working ninety-hour weeks and even sleeping at the office. We told ourselves that we surely would not need to go to such lengths. Anyway, we thought that all this frantic last-minute effort indicated more a Japanese variety of the type "A" personality than anything else.

About six months after our trip to JUSE in late 1985, the word came back to us that JUSE's governing board had decided that a company like FPL could apply for the Deming Prize; but since there were no protocols or procedures in place for overseas companies, these would have to be developed before an application could be accepted. Shortly thereafter they appointed a committee to work on these matters. In about a year we received a draft of the new overseas procedures and were asked to provide our comments on them.

One of our first concerns was the enormous need for translators and interpreters. JUSE's first proposal required that almost everything, both written and oral, be in Japanese. This requirement was later greatly reduced; otherwise, frankly, I don't know how we could have done it. We knew that there was not even one interpreter qualified for this kind of work in all of South Florida. The highly technical nature of the terminology made communication more complex, even among people who all spoke English, much less between Japanese and English. We had located a few interpreters in Japan who could do this type of work, but the ones we had in Florida were still learning. We had a stroke of good fortune when, in 1987, Ms. Noriko Hosoyamada, who was the best of all the interpreters we had been able to find, agreed to come to work for FPL in Miami.

The Deming Prize procedures called for sending an application to JUSE in November announcing a desire to apply for the prize the following year. If this was approved, the next step was to prepare a description of QIP itself, a very detailed and thorough description of the quality improvement activities for every division, department, and plant in the company. In all, as it worked out, the company was broken down into eight separate units, each of which would need to provide its own description of its quality improvement activities. This description was comprised largely of data, charts, and graphs, with relatively little text.

If the written description of QIP passed its review, we would be so notified and asked to meet with a working group which would address the issues of dates, schedules, procedures, interpreter requirements, etc., for the ensuing audit.

After these matters were worked out, the next step would be the on-site audit. We were told that in our case two weeks would be needed to complete the audit. Finally, a very tense two-month period would follow while we waited to find out if we had won. We were beginning to understand what a massive undertaking it was going to be.

Once our counselors were assisting us, our intensity in implementing TQM grew. Our counselors tended to specialize. Dr. Kano worked primarily with the five divisions in the area of customer service; Dr. Makabe's area was the power plants; and Dr. Kondo expended most of his efforts with the General Office departments. Dr. Asaka was the chief counselor over the entire effort.

In general, the counselors visited FPL for a week at a time to work intensively with the part of the company in which they were interested. Typically, they conducted a series of clinics during which various departments made presentations on their QIP efforts (i.e., their QI stories). The clinics were also attended by a large audience of people from the other departments in the area.

Following the presentations, the counselors asked a series of questions intended to highlight the weak points in the QI story. It was an unfamiliar teaching style for us, and it took us a while to learn how it worked.

We held two steering committee meetings in Japan in 1986 and two more in 1987. A number of FPL study missions also traveled to Japan during these two years. In 1986, we focused on installing Policy Management; in 1987, we concentrated on Quality in Daily Work; and in 1988 we tried to boost our performance overall to prepare ourselves for the final challenge.

Whenever our people were in Japan, we tried to arrange for them to visit Deming Prize winners, especially those companies that were part of an American organization. The three we visited repeatedly were Fuji-Xerox, Yokogawa Hewlett-Packard, and the Texas Instruments plant in Oita. But we always ended the trips with a visit to Kansai Electric Power Company, whose help was invaluable. How these companies put up with so many visits by our people I will never know. But then, they understood better than we did what lay ahead for us. Having been there themselves, they were utterly patient with us and never refused to help. It was as if we had passed our initiation test and were now part of an inside group.

We also had an arrangement with Kansai Power Company to exchange employees. I remember telling Kazuhiko Kato, a Kansai engineer who was with us during 1989, that there had to be a special place in heaven for anyone who went through the Deming challenge and audit twice!

Somehow, very early on, the rumor got around that we wanted to challenge for the Deming Prize. One way or another, on every visit the conversation came around to that subject. When we said we hoped to be good enough someday to go for the prize, everyone's eyes would open wide, and with a touch of sympathetic concern in their voices they would shake our hands and wish us luck. That should have told us something.

After our steering committee meeting early in 1988, Dr. Asaka and I discussed the timing for our challenge. For a number of reasons, I still felt that 1989 was the best year for FPL. Dr. Asaka agreed. When we returned from Japan, I talked to each of the officers of the company and got their assurance of full support for the Deming challenge. Some were more enthusiastic than others, but each one said that we should go for it and that neither they nor their departments would let the rest of the company down.

I also discussed our desire to challenge for the Deming Prize with the FPL Board of Directors. It was my practice from time to time throughout our implementation of QIP to inform the board of our progress, primarily by reporting to them on our results. As usual, the board supported anything management felt would strengthen the company. In fact, the chairman of the board of FPL Group (our holding company), the same Marshall McDonald who had started us in QIP, asked me to name the first man to run the four-minute mile. I replied, "Roger Bannister." Then he asked who the second man was, to which I answered, "I don't know." He said we should not only go for the prize, but be the first Americans to do so.

Without discussing the Deming challenge with anyone else, public or private, we began to pick up the tempo. An air of urgency and excitement entered into our plans and our people began to sense it.

Each of our counselors, except Dr. Asaka, had been coming to FPL to hold clinics once or twice a year. Now they began to visit three or four times a year and stayed for up to two weeks. In addition, two junior counselors, Mr. Yukihiro Ando and Dr. Kazuyuki Suzuki, were spending a good deal of time working with smaller groups of employees to improve their QIP skills. The junior counselors' involvement with the specifics of problem solving, as well as their more familiar teaching style, made them great favorites with our employees.

As the officers' periodic reviews of how we were doing in reaching our quality goals and targets intensified, everyone started to realize that we were putting a very high priority on achieving good results. The process used to obtain the results was also gone over in great detail so that we could be certain that the cause and effect relationship in problem solving was logical and consistent. The vendor quality program accelerated, and all through FPL, things began to pulse and take on added meaning.

The pressure was beginning to build on all of us as we began to prepare for the October 1988 meeting of the steering committee. Our plan was to have one of the proposed Deming audit units make a presentation, which we intended to be a model of our description of QIP to JUSE. The Power Resources Department (fossil power plants) was chosen to make this presentation. At that point, they seemed to us to have the best overall story to tell.

The department worked long and hard to prepare its presentation. We reviewed each of the four presentations that made up their overall quality improvement story over and over. It seemed to us to be a clear and powerful example of how the process was being used to obtain very positive results. When we left for Japan we felt very good about our progress and the QI story we were going to show to the steering committee.

The steering committee meeting was a disaster. In our prior meetings with Dr. Asaka, he typically took the very best story and pointed out its weaknesses. He always selected the candidates for his critical analysis very carefully. I noticed that he never picked out anyone at a low level in the organization or anyone who seemed somehow vulnerable or easily hurt. Indeed, a sort of perverse pride came to be associated with being chosen for Dr. Asaka's critique.

This time, however, Dr. Asaka went over all four presentations with a fine-tooth comb. Each and every flaw was pointed out until nothing seemed left to criticize.

Dr. Asaka very much wanted us to do well and was disappointed in our progress, to say the least. Our head coach was getting a little nervous as the championship game drew near, and the tension was showing. He was so upset that I thought he might tell us we just were not ready to challenge in 1989. When I met privately with Dr. Asaka after the steering committee meeting, he told me we had missed the whole point of the master quality improvement story and that top management's focus should be on the forest, not on each tree. What we had shown him was a series of four department-level QI stories, not a corporate-level master QI story. Then he came down hard on the point that we had a great deal of work to do to get the description of QIP ready. Finally, he emphasized the responsibility of myself, our president Bob Tallon, and the other officers to the entire company. We came home crestfallen but determined to improve. In fact, we called FPL before we left Japan to pass on what we had learned, so as not to lose any time.

For the next month the phone rang constantly as Dr. Asaka thought of more things he wanted us to work on. Our other counselors were also pressed to do a better job of teaching us. I still don't know what Dr. Asaka said to them privately, but we could sense the tension in them also. I got the feeling that he was much harder on them than he was on us. In fact, at times I wondered why they were willing to go through all this. After all, they were very prominent in their own right. But then, why were any of us so absolutely determined to succeed? Dr. Asaka knows people. He knew how to motivate us all. He absolutely believed we were capable of implementing a total quality management system. In a real sense he had chosen us, not we him. Indeed, he thought we were better than we had ever dreamed we could be, and no one wanted to be the one to let him down. By his confidence in us, Dr. Asaka was teaching us a lesson about respect for people in the most profound way.

At FPL the quality improvement process is, and has been from the beginning, a line responsibility. The Quality Improvement Department has been deliberately kept small. As a result of the October 1988 steering committee meeting, I realized that while this small department was the proper organization for implementing quality at FPL, it was not the best one for something like the challenge for the Deming Prize.

You might say we needed a master pilot to navigate us through the difficult passage of the Deming challenge. I decided to select one of our top officers to lead the Deming project. It seemed to me that Wayne Brunetti, one of our two executive vice presidents, had the right experience for this task. By appointing an officer at that level in the company, I was also sending a clear message of how important the Deming challenge was.

Accordingly, I announced to all of the employees that we were challenging for the Deming Prize and that, for the duration, Wayne would be relieved of all other duties and would be in overall charge of the Deming Prize effort. The first major task we faced was to put together the description of QIP.

First we mailed our six-page application to JUSE announcing

our desire to challenge for the Deming Prize in November of 1988. In December we received notice from JUSE that our application had been accepted. Now we had six weeks to complete the description of our quality improvement process. The entire description had ten parts: an overall corporate description of QIP followed by eight separate unit descriptions and a glossary of terms. The eight units consisted of the five regional divisions of the company, the fossil power plants, the nuclear power plants, and finally the twenty-one General Office departments.

While they had already started at this time, each element of the company or audit unit now went to work in earnest to put together their part of the "Description of QIP" (DQIP). Since they are all similar, the five regional divisions had the advantage of borrowing ideas from one another. Both the nuclear and fossil power plants had very good results to point out, which helped them focus their descriptions. The General Office description was tough—twenty-one departments in about ninety pages. Each department had to condense four years of activities into four pages. We reluctantly decided that they had to choose only the most significant thing each department had done for inclusion in the DQIP. And then there was still the overall corporate description of QIP. Basically, the top six officers had to put this together ourselves. We had learned that this task could not be delegated. Nobody else could do it and just hand it to us; it had to be our story. We had to understand every word, chart, and graph, and be able to answer the "five why" questions—a procedure in which the question "why?" is asked five times in succession—about everything we said.

While each of us prepared our own part of the corporate description of QIP, our work was constantly reviewed, over and over, by others. We asked for suggestions from anyone we thought could help us. At times we threw out entire sections of our work and started all over again. But each one of us was deeply involved in the process throughout, and we tried to help each other as much as we could.

Our counselors assisted us, as did people from Kansai Electric. They pointed out omissions and weak points but were very careful not to put words in our mouths. It had to be our story.

The completed QIP description contained almost 1,000 pages. We could have used many more, but this was the limit set by JUSE. About one-third of the space was text and the other two-thirds were charts, graphs, and diagrams.

The various versions of the description were fed to the translators for translation into Japanese as we went along. This was not the most efficient way to do it because of our constant, extensive revisions, but we were running out of time. We employed a number of translators with various degrees of skill. The rough translation was done by the less skilled and the final proofing and editing was given to our chief translator. Because the DQIP was mostly graphs, charts, and technical terms, it was a complex job, but it was done on time and very competently. And then off to the printer the whole thing went.

In January, and on schedule, the DQIP was filed with JUSE in Tokyo. It had been a tremendous effort but there was no time for rest. Although it would be two months before we would know if our description of QIP had passed, we had to make the most of every minute left to us in the meantime to get ready for the audit.

We had met most of our quality improvement goals in 1988, but we had set even more ambitious goals for 1989. We wanted to be able to show continuing progress to the examiners; and in the areas of teams, vendors, statistical quality control, and suggestions, we had a lot of work to do to sustain the momentum.

In addition to all this, a totally new task loomed before us: preparing for the examination itself. The preparation of the DQIP had been limited to relatively few managers and staff. Preparation for the exam would involve just about everyone. We knew that top management, both nuclear plants, and all twenty-one General Office departments were almost certain to be examined. Not every division or plant would be examined, but we did not know which would and which would not. We therefore could not limit our preparation in any way. Of course, this was the purpose of the challenge—to perfect our quality improvement skills company-wide. We therefore intended to keep everyone under the gun so that the entire company would make improvements in QIP. There were to be no second-class citizens.

The audit itself would consist of several parts. "Schedule A" would be the time when the company could tell its story. Each unit executive would have the opportunity at the beginning of the unit audit to point out the highlights and successes of that unit, including any demonstrations in the field or office of notable strong points. Each Schedule A presentation would be followed by a question-and-answer period.

"Schedule B," the examiners' part of the audit, would take up about two-thirds of the total exam time. During this segment the examiners would question each work group on anything they chose. In order to get full credit, the person answering the question had to answer with data, and would be expected to produce the supporting data within three minutes. This phase of the exam would test how thoroughly the company was applying quality improvement practices at all levels.

During a general session held at the end of each unit's Schedule B exam, the company would have a chance to augment any answers that needed to be improved. This session would also allow the examiners one final chance to ask any questions they might forget to ask the first time or to clear up any conflicting answers they had received.

On the last day of the audit, four other officers and I would give a general presentation on the overall company, which would include a closing question-and-answer period. This would serve as the overall wrapup general session for the audit.

But the last hour of the audit would be spent in a closed-session meeting of the unit executives and other top officers with the examiners. We were never told how to prepare for this part.

The other officers and I began to prepare our formal Schedule A presentations, simultaneously trying to think of every question that might be asked. During this period, we fired off one list of questions after another to be researched for answers. For the Schedule B presentations every area of the company needed to be ready for an audit. This was a full-court press, and the hours we all worked began to grow longer and longer.

The requirement we placed on ourselves was to have each and every work section in the company able to make a presentation to the examiners. Somewhere between one and five people in each section might be called on to stand before the examiner and answer questions. Since there were about 200 such sections, over 1,000 people needed to be ready to stand up and describe our quality improvement system and their part in it. Each presenter had to be supported by two or three others who would produce the necessary data to back up answers. Of course, the examiners might stop and ask anyone they saw questions about what they did to support the company's quality improvement efforts, so many other employees sat in and listened to the Schedule B practice presentations. Getting ready was going to be a big, big job.

Of course, it was too much for a small group to do on its own. Everyone had to help everyone else in any way they could.

Our practice schedule called for each section to make a one-hour presentation once a month, usually on the weekends. The presentation would be reviewed by the section's manager and managers from two other departments. We would look at first one aspect of QIP, then another—for example, policy management, education and training, team activity, control systems, and so on. A great deal of effort went into preparing for these practice presentations. When a department developed a good reputation for its presentations, the audience was filled with people from other departments who came to observe and learn.

As the audit drew nearer, we held reviews every other Saturday—half the company one week and the other half the next. The officers tried to attend as many of these as possible, but in the main the managers had to help each other, like a rising tide lifting all boats.

In 1989 all of our counselors, including Dr. Asaka for the first time, came over for a week on two different occasions. They worked with us very intently to improve our application and understanding of the process, although we were somewhat disappointed that they did not give us much direction on how to improve our audit presentation skills. This may have been due to their academic background: their ethics as teachers would not let them teach test-taking skills. During this period, Kansai Electric also sent over some senior people from time to time to help us when we ran into problems.

In the first go-round of reviews, about one-third of the managers did fair and another third were nothing short of poor. The rest were somewhere in between. We learned by this means that some of our managers had not personally taken a leadership role in QIP, as became very evident when they stood up and tried to describe their department's activities. They just stood there with egg on their faces, unable to explain what their departments did to support the corporate quality improvement goals and unable to answer very many questions.

Displaying their inadequacies before people from all over the company, including many of their own employees, was very embarrassing for these managers, to put it mildly. Our approach, however, was not to give them hell but to give them help. The rest of us could well remember the time when we went through the same experience. To their credit, they all pulled up their socks and did much better the second time around. In fact, a few of them improved so much, we thought they might have passed the audit itself. But we didn't let up on anyone; we just raised the expected standards the next time around. Just to meet the minimum score would be too risky. We knew we needed some departments to do very well to give us a margin of safety.

Schedule B practice sessions consisted of five-minute descriptions of the department, its purpose, and its progress, presented by the department manager, who requested questions when he or she was done. Overall, these Schedule B sessions would run for one to two hours. When a question was asked, the manager decided who was best qualified to answer. Sometimes the managers answered themselves, but most often one of the supervisors or assistant managers was asked to answer. From the start, we wanted the answer to be supported with data and asked that those supporting the presenter have the data in front of the examiner within the required three minutes.

We thought each manager knew his or her department's role in supporting the company and the quality improvement process, and we thought this had been made very clear to all their employees. But again, through our practice sessions for Schedule B we learned that this just was not so. I don't think we were very different from other companies in this respect. We all assume too much. As we went through this practice process over and over, however, everything began to become very clear—what the departments did, the order of importance of what they did, how they measured their progress, what their goals were, how they were doing in meeting those goals, how QIP was used to assist in this, and what their plans for the future were. Every aspect of every department's and work section's quality improvement process was discussed over and over before an audience made up of the principal support groups for each manager and other managers from all over the company.

It wasn't just the first-level managers who went through this same drill, but all the officers of the company, including myself. In times past, people have told me that what went on inside my head was something of a mystery to them. I could never understand why, but as I practiced my own presentation before an audience of employees I realized that I wasn't all that clear in describing what I felt we ought to do well and what kind of an external business environment I thought we would be facing. I improved in this, together with everyone else. The process Dr. Asaka had described as "aligning the vectors" was taking place right before our eyes. We now knew why those companies that had won the Deming Prize had made so much more progress than those that had not. No matter what you may tell yourself, you just would not endure this kind of effort if you were not staring the exam in the face.

In March we were notified that our description of quality improvement had passed. Our attendance was requested at a May meeting in Tokyo with our examiners, so that we could provide them with a general overview of the company prior to the audit itself. This would allow the examiners to concentrate their time in Florida at the company on the actual audit. Many issues relating to schedules, travel, and arrangements also had to be discussed in advance of the actual audit.

We asked for permission to present a videotape showing FPL's facilities and service territory, and presenting facts about the company and its history. We received permission, and prepared the video, which FPL still shows as part of new employees' initial orientation to the company.

Our biggest problem in getting ready for this meeting was that it came at a time when we were very busy with all the other preparation activity. But Wayne Brunetti and the Quality Improvement Department managed the situation well, and we were ready and able to show up at the appointed time in Tokyo. While this meeting was absolutely not part of the audit, we certainly wanted to make a good impression, and it was our first opportunity to stand before the examiners and size up one another.

We were familiar with a few of the examiners already. Dr. Yoji Akao and Dr. Hitoshi Kume we knew from their books. And we had met most of the examiners at one or more quality conferences we had attended in Japan and the United States. Dr. Ikuro Kusaba, the lead examiner, had also been to FPL for four days early in 1984. At that time, we had asked him to assess where we were in our QIP implementation. In his report to us after his tour of the company, he had described our level of QIP as primitive—only the first of many times our balloon was popped. We certainly hoped we would be able to change his assessment of us this time.

The presentations in Tokyo seemed to go well. The questions we got were just for clarification, the examiners seemed friendly, and we made some good progress on the administrative matters as well. Even though we knew we had five hard months ahead of us, we returned from our first meeting with the examiners feeling good.

# The Deming Prize Preparation, Part 2

**W**hen we returned from the May meeting in Tokyo with the examiners, we faced a whole new set of problems. Up until that time our activities had been in direct support of the implementation of our quality system. Now, in addition to those continuing efforts we had to master a host of administrative details in connection with the exam. All vacations were canceled for the duration.

We certainly had to make the substance of our story as strong as possible, but on the other hand, we did not want to flop on our faces because of sloppy administration. It was time to worry about details like presentation rooms, layouts, audiovisual equipment, support rooms, telephones, and travel.

Then there was the question of organizing the support the presenters needed. We needed people to record the questions and answers, and to analyze the answers to see if they needed to be corrected or expanded. Mountains of backup data had to be produced and filed so that information could be retrieved in seconds. The different departments had started to develop their own ways to handle this issue. For the smaller sections, the most popular method was to use simple milk crate files. As the practice sessions continued, the number of such files grew apace. A good indicator of the extent of practice taking place was the number of such files being trundled through the halls and elevators. The company resembled a giant ant colony with each person carrying about his or her own cargo.

Since the examiners would be able to ask written as well as oral questions, a process had to be in place to receive, record, and answer their written questions. We also wanted to develop a method to inform the person before the examiner about what written questions the examiner was asking. This would give the person some warning of what to expect next. Then, each evening as the exam progressed, all of the answers, written and oral, had to be checked for accuracy and completeness.

Throughout the spring and early summer of 1989 we continued to practice. As we went through the Schedule A practice sessions we had a number of employees attend as observers, partly in order to develop some depth, or bench strength. We wanted a back-up available for each major presenter. In many cases during the audit, we took the most knowledgeable of these back-ups and assigned them the task of checking all answers for completeness and accuracy.

When a written question was asked by someone playing the role of examiner, it was taken to the support room by messenger. There it was handed to a dispatcher who logged in the question and directed it to the group that had the appropriate files of information. After the material had been retrieved from the files, the person checking answers quickly looked it over to see if they felt it answered the question. If it did, it was sent back to the dispatcher, logged out, and then sent to the examiner. By this method we developed our skills at producing the data on answers to written questions in just minutes. The same process was used to support employees answering oral questions during the Schedule B exams.

We had yet to devise a procedure to verify oral answers. We had begun videotaping each practice. Both in real time and later by viewing the tapes, the answers were reviewed and critiqued. This was most useful to those who were going to be making presentations, because they could perform a plan-do-check-act cycle on themselves. Since everyone was working on the same goals, an enormous amount of teamwork and cooperation developed during this time. Everyone's suggestions on how things could be improved were listened to with respect. Then we practiced, practiced again—and practiced some more. When you are going for the gold, you can't be too good.

One problem at this time was that we did not know as yet where the examiners would choose to go, so we had to make some guesses. Since the examination would be taking place all over Florida, we needed a group to start planning transportation and lodging. Meals had to be arranged not just for the examiners and their interpreters but also for all the FPL employees who would be involved.

We were becoming very sensitive to schedules and timing. Every event had to start and end on time. This placed a heavy burden on those responsible for transportation, an area in which so many things could go wrong so easily. Most of the longer trips the examiners would make would take place in the evenings, so time wasn't quite so critical for those trips. However, they had to arrive at the examination rooms on time, and all movement from one site to another had to be accomplished on schedule.

Those people responsible for transportation practiced and

timed each segment and worked out alternate routes and back-up plans until they had developed a system that gave them a high probability of meeting their schedules.

Meals and hotels were checked out and planned for with equal fastidiousness. We were instructed not to provide lavish accommodations for the examiners, but we wanted the rooms to be clean and comfortable.

We also had to arrange for elaborate field demonstrations to be laid out and set up. We began to set up a demonstration of our computer capability in the General Office atrium. The Miami Division and the two nuclear plants were almost sure to be examined, so they began to arrange field demonstrations of some of their quality improvement successes. People had to be trained to describe the demonstrations to the examiners, so a whole new group of employees began to practice presentations.

Another major task was locating a total of about forty rather large rooms throughout the company for possible use as examinations rooms. As it turned out, we actually used twenty-three of these preselected rooms during the exam. Each room had to have access to an area nearby that could be used by the back-up and support personnel. Once we located these areas, it was then necessary to equip them with audiovisual equipment, including provisions for the necessary videotaping equipment. FPL has its own fiber optics systems, and where possible, we wanted our employees to be able to watch some of the exam while it was in progress. This turned out to be very useful to those who were yet to be examined. By seeing how the exam went, they were able to psych themselves up and get emotionally prepared. As the exam itself took place, we discovered that we had our own TV stars. They became overnight heros.

We began to use these areas for our practice sessions to shake down any problems. Most of these areas continue to be used today for presentations. In fact, much of the effort we spent getting ready for the exam has had lasting benefits.

Each process that had to take place was flow charted to ensure that nothing fell through the cracks. A large number of our people had to be selected and trained for their roles during the exam—people with temporary new job titles like master of ceremonies, timekeeper, director of support room, document exit checker, and so on. In all, there were twenty-three such titles.

Most of this effort was taking place on the weekends. I realized just how much this was so when someone informed me that our cafeteria was serving more meals on Saturdays and Sundays than it was on weekdays.

A task that was critical to our success or failure was interpretation. Ms. Hosoyamada had been recruiting other interpreters ever since she started working with FPL. She had been able to locate a few with promise in Japan, California, and the Washington, D.C. area. We used her recruits to interpret when the counselors held their clinics at FPL and at the steering committee meetings. In this manner, they learned the terminology of the electric utility industry and QIP. Some were only used once but gradually a small group of about six very good translators were selected and given considerable experience. To ensure consistency of translation, we held some formal training classes on the most difficult terms just before the exam. And to improve their hands-on knowledge, the interpreters were taken on some field trips to power plants and other areas of the company. This effort paid off; one interpreter was assigned to each examiner for the duration of the exam, and they all came through like the professionals they are.

This was the testing time in more ways than one. If a person was not carrying his or her weight, someone else had to be found to get the job done, and quickly. Happily, there were not very many people who didn't come through. All sorts of people at all levels in the company stepped up to the task at hand. It was a time to make a reputation for yourself and to develop self-confidence. Some people thrived on it, doing everything that was asked of them and then some. As our people hurried about their tasks during this period, a new spirit surfaced—a feeling of excitement and energy in the air. No one wanted to be left out of what was happening. It was serious work and yet it was also exhilarating—fun.

# What Else Can Go Wrong?

*Y*ou might say that things were getting busy. I was working at least ten hours a day and seven days a week. But then so were a lot of other people. There were so many cars in the parking lot at the General Office on the weekend that our employees had to carpool. So much for my theory about a Japanese type "A" personality!

And as if all this were not enough, we had scheduled two clinics with our counselors just before the exam, one in May and another in June. The May clinic would be the first time Dr. Asaka had ever been to FPL. Moreover, our friends in Japan who had been through it told us these would be the toughest clinics of all.

We treated these two clinics like dry runs for the Deming exam. Since we were spending all our time getting ready for the exam, we had no time left to get ready for the clinics separately. Besides, we considered the clinics a good opportunity to put ourselves through a dress rehearsal.

As the clinics began we noticed something right away. Dr. Asaka and the other counselors were nothing like we had imagined they would be. Instead of tough and stern, they were calm and friendly. Their manner was much like that of a helpful coach watching and suggesting little improvements, encouraging, and praising. Dr. Asaka especially gave strong encouragement and support to team members and first-line employees. We even have a photograph of Dr. Asaka taken at this time with an enormous smile on his face. Our employees began to lose some of their nervousness, and even started to ask Dr. Asaka to autograph their presentation papers. I watched all this in utter amazement. I learned something new from Dr. Asaka every time I was with him.

We knew that Dr. Asaka had a history of high blood pressure and poor health in general. On Wednesday of the first clinic, he began to feel ill. When I heard this, I assure you that I began to do some fervent praying. Ms. Hosoyomada had anticipated that something like this might happen. She had previously contacted both Dr. Asaka's doctor and his wife to obtain his medical history and a list of his prescriptions, which she had placed in the hands of a heart specialist in Miami. As it turned out, we didn't need to use these plans. When Dr. Asaka announced the next day that he felt fine, a lot of other people also felt much better.

The first clinic ended with a long list of things we needed to improve, but it had been good practice for all of us and instilled in us new self-confidence.

About this time, however, some things began to go from bad to worse at FPL. For years we had been experiencing one problem after another at our Turkey Point Nuclear Plants, some of the earliest nuclear plants built in America. After the 1979 incident at the Three Mile Island nuclear plant in Pennsylvania, these older plants were hit with a large number of additional safety regulations, many of which required the rebuilding of major parts of the plants to meet the new safety standards. As we tried to carry out the rebuilding while still operating the plants, we encountered many difficulties. Just as we got one problem behind us, a new one always seemed to appear.

Because of this heavy workload, in 1988 the Turkey Point personnel were not as advanced in the application of QIP as most of the rest of the company. But I felt things were getting better at Turkey Point and that they would have time to catch up in late 1988 and early 1989. Unfortunately, it didn't work out this way; they never got a breathing spell.

Near the end of 1988 we were confronted with a host of allegations of safety violations at Turkey Point made to the Nuclear Regulatory Commission by a discharged employee. We were able to answer these allegations successfully but doing so took an enormous amount of time and effort, and this burden fell largely on the managers at the plant.

Then both plants were taken out of service for a scheduled refueling and maintenance outage. A dual plant outage was always a very difficult period for the plant personnel to manage. On this occasion, we did not even come close to returning the plants to operation on schedule. Instead, we found one problem after another that had to be fixed first.

Then, we were hit by a new crisis when almost half of the licensed operators of the plant failed to pass a scheduled, periodic requalification exam. They had to enter into a period of intense study before being retested. Every one of them passed the second time around, but it was another major diversion of management resources that clearly took precedence over the Quality Improvement Program. The people at the plant were successfully coping with these problems one after the other, and they were even making some progress with QIP, but not fast enough. We were running out of time.

Finally, one of the plants returned to operation and things seemed to improve. I decided to make a trip to Turkey Point to see how they were coming along with QIP and to give them some encouragement. I was encouraged by what I saw—they seemed to have high morale, especially given all they had just been through.

A few days later, Marshall McDonald, the chairman of FPL Group, and the man who had started us in all this, asked me about our plans if we failed to win the Deming Prize. Something about the way he said this seemed strange to me. I asked him if he knew something that I didn't know. He replied, "Oh, no." I didn't really believe him. By the time we finished this conversation I sensed that he was washing his hands of the Deming challenge and that it was my head on the block if we failed.

But I had too many other things to worry about to even consider failure. Later, I made several more visits to Turkey Point and found things strongly improving there. I was sure they would be ready for the Deming exam and they were the ones I had been most worried about. The rest of the company was improving very fast and I was beginning to feel better and better.

Then the roof fell in. About 7:30 one morning late in May, shortly after I arrived at work, I received a call from the local U.S. Attorney. He announced that there was an ongoing investigation of drug trafficking at Turkey Point. Four sealed indictments had been issued ordering the arrest of, among others, some of our employees at Turkey Point. He could not tell me the names until the arrests were made, but said that later that morning a press conference would be held to disclose what they had found about a drug problem at Turkey Point. I was stunned.

There had been rumors of drug use at both FPL and Turkey Point for years. We had taken numerous steps to counteract any drug use, including about six months earlier, instituting a random drug-testing program at all our nuclear plants. A few employees tested positive, but the number was quite small.

We began to notify everyone who needed to know: various governmental agencies, the media, our board of directors, and numerous FPL employees were informed. When the names of those arrested were announced later that morning, it turned out that only one of them was an FPL employee. And while he was at Turkey Point, he did not work at the nuclear plant. One of the others arrested had worked for a contractor at the plant at an earlier time.

The evening news on television was awful. I am sure viewers believed that Turkey Point was a pit of corruption. And there were all sorts of hints that there was much more to be revealed later. The morning papers were just as damning. In the meantime many of our employees had volunteered the information that they had been questioned that night by the FBI.

In our preparation for the Deming Prize we had tried to think of everything that could happen. We had all kinds of contingency plans, but this was one thing we did not imagine. I have come to learn that something unexpected will inevitably happen.

The media reports indicating that there were deeper secrets to be revealed were our biggest problem. We didn't know where we stood. We didn't have the facts. Of course, the antinuclear crowd were in full cry, calling for the plant's closing. Even those editors who were in favor of nuclear power were questioning whether Turkey Point should be allowed to continue to operate.

The morale at the plant fell through the floor. No one knew who of their fellow workers might be involved. Suspicion and distrust were rampant. We could kiss the Deming Prize goodbye if we didn't do something fast, but if we couldn't recover from this problem the failure to win the Deming Prize was not going to be our biggest worry. The reliability of the electric system in South Florida could be in jeopardy, and the company's financial health could be ruined for years. In all of my thirty-seven years at FPL I could not remember a greater crisis.

In the days following, the rumors continued to fly. As I looked around, our friends seemed few and far between. We did have some left and I will never forget who they are! And we were not without resources. We had our own employees, and I had faith in them. By this time their initial dismay had started to turn into anger. We had formed a council of war the first day. One of our priorities was to clear the names of the employees who were not drug users. Accordingly, we started a massive drug-testing program. The officers, including myself, and all the managers at the plant submitted to a drug test. There had been some speculation in the media that the licensed operators of the plant might be involved. We were pleased when they demanded that they be tested, and of course, they all tested clean. Then the president of our local IBEW, who heretofore had opposed some of the drug-testing programs, showed up at the plant gate (he was not an employee at Turkey Point) and insisted that he be tested for drugs and urged all of the union employees there to follow his example. I always did respect that man. We put together a priority list of those jobs that were most critical to the plant and began a 100 percent drug-testing program, starting at the top of the list. One of our problems was that those who were not at the top of the list didn't want to wait, but the lab we were using was only capable of processing about 400 tests per day.

Over 2,500 people ultimately took the test, so most just had to wait their turn. One employee refused to take the test and subsequently left the company. Then as the test reports began to come back, they were most gratifying. It turned out that we must have had one of the most drug-free workplaces in America. Only a tiny handful tested positive. (They went into a rehab program.) As the negative reports came back, we could see the pride return on everyone's faces, but most of all, as each employee was cleared, his or her back straightened and shoulders squared and the old pride visibly returned.

The testing program wasn't the only thing we had to do during this period—we had to be in constant contact with the media. The story went all over the world, including to Japan. We also were obliged to assist the U.S. Attorney and the FBI in their investigation. It goes without saying that the Nuclear Regulatory Commission had a keen interest in the matter, and their needs had to be met as well. In the end, the NRC told us that our handling of the drug issue ultimately worked to our favor because it put to bed the rumors about drug use at Turkey Point. All in all, a lot of people were by now working ninety-hour weeks and sleeping at the office.

The employees were not able to do much on QIP while all of this drug flap was going on at the plant. First things first, after all. But as things began to return to normal, I needed to know if the people at Turkey Point were ready to pick up the pieces on QIP or if they were burned out. I set up a Saturday meeting of all the managers at the plant. We had been criticized by our regulators for working the Turkey Point employees too long hours, but Saturday it had to be. We had a straight-from-the-shoulder, free-wheeling discussion about QIP and the Deming Prize challenge, in addition to all of their other problems. Finally I put it to them: I said that the safe and successful operation of the plant was the first priority and the Deming challenge was a distant second. Could they do both? If they felt they could not cope with the Deming challenge and successfully run the plant, they should say the word and I would call off the Deming challenge on the spot. And I meant it.

There was a rather pregnant pause, and then we went around the room and asked each one to say what he or she thought.

I knew what this group had been through and I had no idea how the answers would come out. The actual words used varied but the answer was invariably a strong, "Hell yes, we can do it.

We're not about to let down our plant or the company. Go for it!" I took their answer at face value and we continued with the challenge, but we all knew that there was a lot of work left to be done. I was very proud to work with people like them. I was also determined that neither the rest of the company nor I was going to let them down either. All this panic had taken place in just two weeks, but it seemed like ten years.

The following week a few of us had to rush over to Tokyo again to work out the last of the protocols and schedules with the examiners. Since I was sure the examiners had heard about our problems at Turkey Point, I gave them some information about the matter, focusing on how well the results of the drug testing were coming out. I was sure they were saying to themselves, "Only in America!" But the meeting went very well and then we were on our way back to Miami.

When I returned in June, we had only four days to go before our counselors were due to arrive for their final clinic before the exam. If I or they felt that Florida Power & Light could not pass the exam, it was our duty to tell JUSE. I was determined that the people of FPL should get their chance to go for the prize, but that might not be good enough. I had never been through a Deming exam, and I didn't know how the drug problem might have affected our chances. I had to be very open with the counselors about this issue because I needed their counsel as never before. Also, as I went about the General Office I noticed that some of the lilt had gone out of the step of those who scurried about their tasks. For some reason the rest of the company had gone into the dumps.

It was my responsibility to make the opening statement at this last clinic before the exam. Suddenly that seemed more important than ever. I lay awake two nights thinking about what I should say.

The clinic was to be televised over our in-house network,

allowing about 60 percent of our employees to watch and hear what I said live; the rest would see it on tape. It was an opportunity for me to live up to the trust and responsibility that had been placed in me. I decided to address principally the employees of FPL, and not the counselors. The counselors could judge us just as we were.

I had twenty minutes to say the most important words of my lifetime of work at FPL. I started by talking about what an honorable and fine company FPL was. I talked about quality and customer satisfaction and how much progress we had made toward being the best electric utility in America. Then I asked them to keep their health as we went through the final months of the Deming challenge, and I said I thought we would win the prize. Finally I talked to the employees of Turkey Point (who were also watching) and told them how proud of them I was, and that every other FPL employee should be too. I closed with the charge to all of our people to do their best. Moreover, I told them they were the best of the best in all of America and they had been able to do something very extraordinary at FPL. In the most important ways they were already winners.

As I went back to my office after the opening session, I saw smiles on all the faces. The old spring was back in their steps. Later I was told that everyone was afraid I was going to announce that we had abandoned our quest to be the best and to win the Deming Prize. Our people were on cloud nine because I had said we were going forward. They had never doubted themselves. It was my courage that had been in question. This time it was I who was being tested, not them. Also the things I had said to the people at Turkey Point seemed to be well received. I was later told that there was a crowd around each of the TV monitors at the plant and when I expressed full confidence in them, there was cheering.

The rest of the clinic also seemed to go well. There was a

good measure of criticism, but everyone was so eager to improve that they all took it in the best possible way.

This was our last contact with our counselors until after the exam. Under the Deming rules they could not contact us any more until after the examination was over. As they got on the plane to leave, we felt a little like the student pilot who is told to solo for the first time—very much alone.

In the wake of the drug crisis, I had talked to the members of our board of directors about how the drug testing and other related matters were going. Gradually they seemed to be feeling better, along with the rest of us, about our progress at Turkey Point. I had not, however, talked to them about the Deming challenge for several months. At our board meeting in June I was somewhat dismayed to find out that there was considerable sentiment among some of the board members to abandon the Deming challenge. I didn't know who had been talking to them or what they had been hearing, but it wasn't good. For five years they had been all for it; now with only weeks to go, there was doubt. After considerable discussions, the decision was made to go forward, but there sure wasn't much enthusiasm on the board anymore. Well, as President Truman said, "If you can't stand the heat, get out of the kitchen."

With four weeks to go, we learned which units would be audited. Those divisions and power plants that were not going to be audited were genuinely disappointed. As it turned out, some of those units we thought were strong and some we felt less sure about were chosen. The JUSE working group had selected a true cross-section of FPL.

It was only at this late date that Wayne Brunetti moved any people around between units. Some of the better people from those units that were not going to be audited were called on to help the others get ready. Also, a few specialists in various aspects of the process were moved to places where they could assist others in supporting roles.

The examination rooms could now be identified, so those responsible for audiovisual and other logistics were able to make final arrangements for equipment and other needs. Travel schedules were finalized and tuned. Some soap and paint were applied here and there, and the place began to look sharp. The scurry and hustle around the office increased. But also the morale was sky-high, more people were smiling and laughing in the halls than ever, and you could sense excitement in the air.

Of course, not everyone was altogether happy with what was going on. During this period I received a couple of unsigned letters from spouses of our employees. They were very critical of the Deming Prize effort and didn't care much for me either. Since I didn't know whom the letters were from, there wasn't much that I could, or felt that I should, do about them.

As we went through the final set of reviews and practice sessions, our people were sharp. They seemed to be able to describe what they did to improve quality smoothly and with data.

But we were still nervous. We could remember other times when we thought we were good and learned to our dismay that we were not so good after all. My own nervousness was showing. I began to roam the halls peering into offices to see if they looked neat. I began to inspect every control chart and QI story hanging on the walls to see that it was perfect. In fact, I was becoming something of a pest.

The fact that we were going for the Deming Prize had received some media coverage. We would have preferred that this hadn't happened. After we won the prize, of course, media coverage would be just fine, but if we didn't win we would be happier if no one talked about it. But since this is America and the media are not to be denied, the fact that we were going for the prize was known beforehand; there was no way we could deny it and maintain our credibility.

One day we came in to find out that we were going to have pickets around the General Office building. Several of the non-FPL South Florida labor unions had decided to stage a sympathy demonstration for the strikers at some West Virginia coal mines. They picked FPL as the site of this demonstration because the new president of FPL Group was on the board of directors of the coal company that was struck. The demonstration came and went without any incidents. However, that got us thinking about a whole array of mischief-making possibilities for which we might need to prepare. Now, there are a few people in the world who are just plain mean. They don't want anyone to succeed at anything. We had even heard of some cases in Japan where there had been efforts to embarrass a company during the Deming exam. We also heard some rumors of certain activities that were planned in our case—sabotage to cause outages, for example. So we did what we could to come up with contingency plans for these kinds of events. As it worked out, none of the rumors was true and we were left alone by those outside the company during the exam. Sometimes we take ourselves too seriously.

Finally with just two weeks to go, Wayne felt we were as ready as we could be. We let everyone have the last two weekends off. To be sure, however, a lot of our people continued to make little last-minute changes. There was just too much nervous energy stored up waiting to be released. We were ready and we were anxious to get started.

# The Exam

*T*he day had finally come. At exactly 9:00 AM on July 24, 1989, the Deming Examiners arrived at the Florida Power & Light offices. As we proceeded through the opening formalities I was proud of all the skills we had acquired over the last four years. If we made any gaffs, I did not see them. The opening ceremonial activities seemed to pass in the blink of an eye and the exam proper began.

The examiners were to work in pairs. This, we were told, was so that if one examiner was very harsh or even unfair, the other would provide a balancing point of view. One FPL interpreter was assigned to each examiner. In addition, they had brought an interpreter of their own, who primarily interpreted for the honcho or chief examiner but also followed the overall exam to verify the accuracy of the other interpreters. This was another check and balance measure. Finally, a representative from the JUSE staff who was also part of the delegation acted as an overall observer to ensure that all the rules and procedures were followed. Not much was left to chance or individual bias. We were assured that these arrangements (with the obvious exception of the interpreters) were the same arrangements that would be used for a Japanese company's exam.

155

For the first week of the exam there were to be two pairs of examiners. Because distances between sites to be covered were greater than would be the case in Japan, it was necessary for the examiners to split up. One pair would examine the nuclear power plants and their staffs while the second pair examined the fossil power plants. And since some of these examiners would not be returning for the second week, it was felt that they should spend half a day each with the customer service part of the company. This would give them a chance to get an overall view of the company's activities.

The schedule for the first day was as follows: one pair of examiners came to the General Office and began the exam of the Nuclear Power Department; the other pair started in the Hialeah Customer Service Office. At noon, they changed locations; the first pair went to the Southern Division Emergency Control Center while the second pair came to the General Office and began the fossil power exam.

My role that first day was limited. I handled the greetings and ceremonies and then was only an observer, spending the day in the presentation room at the General Office. You could say that I had the catbird seat.

The first Schedule A presentations were just as we had practiced: accurate, competent, concise, and on time. But they were delivered in a somewhat uptight, nervous manner. The examiners noticed this and told us to just relax and tell our story. That was easy for them to say—but their saying so did seem to help a little. Of course, the power plant group had very good results to rely on, which also boosted their confidence.

After the Schedule A presentations, the written and oral questions started coming thick and fast. Runners were running. Checkers were checking. Things seemed to be humming on all cylinders. And then I found myself waving goodbye as the examiners left to go back to their hotel. The first day's exam was over, but there was still a lot of work to do.

Upon review, the answers given looked good. In some cases the examiners had asked for additional material to study. These data were assembled so that they could be placed before the examiners first thing the next morning. This became a daily process. On occasion the material was sent to the hotel in the evening but in no case was it made available later than the first thing the next morning. If the examiners looked over all the material they asked for, they must have worked late into every night.

We looked for a pattern or theme in the type of questions asked, and for areas we expected to be covered that had not as yet been broached. Such areas as training or suggestions would certainly be covered, so any open issues in these areas would need to be asked about at a later time. In this manner we could give a little forewarning of what to expect to those yet to be examined. But all of this activity was more useful as therapy than anything else. At this point, the outcome of the exam was very much in the hands of FPL's employees. They were the ones standing in front of the examiners answering questions or supporting the presenters with data. There was little more that top management could do. Whether we passed or failed was up to the thousands of employees involved.

The second day's schedule called for the examiners to travel. One pair went thirty miles south of Miami to the Turkey Point Nuclear Plant while the other one went 150 miles north to the Martin Fossil Plant.

In planning our presentations for the exam, we faced a dilemma: Did we show all of our good points up front, or did we hold back a few goodies and hope we would get the opportunity to let them come out as part of the exam? If we could let a few really good things pop out during the exam, we thought they might have a greater impact. We reasoned that if the examiners had to drag a shining example of quality out of us, they might wonder how many more might be waiting to be discovered. Of course, we ran the risk that we might never get an opening and our good point would remain our own little secret, so we didn't hold back too much.

At the end of the Martin Plant exam, Bill Hensler, the plant manager, was up during the general session wrap-up. He was asked just the question he was looking for and let drop the fact that of the twenty-six electric generators in the world built like the ones at Martin, the two Martin units ranked number one and number five for reliability (EFOR). (Those two units ranked number one and number two in the world by the end of 1989.) Sometimes you lose, but sometimes you win.

The exam at Turkey Point began with a few opening statements followed by a general tour of the plant and several demonstrations. In FPL's new and very elaborate Turkey Point training facility, the most impressive part is the complete computerized replica of the plant's operation control center. The operators of the plant can go to the training control room and safely practice for any emergency conditions that might occur, much like the simulator training used by airline pilots.

The plant had planned to stage a simulated emergency for the examiners. The examiners were warned that there would be a loud noise followed by darkness with alarms and flashing red lights. The drill fizzled. There was no loud noise, no flashing lights (but there were some very red faces going on and off). While the control room personnel regrouped, the examiners were taken through the rest of the training facility to see how the plant personnel are trained. All plant personnel receive periodic training, and the rest of the facility is very impressive in its own right. As they were about to leave to go back to the plant, the examiners were grabbed by the control room trainers and belatedly shown the simulated emergency, which this time worked perfectly.

As one of the examiners was leaving he commented that a clock on the wall in an out-of-the-way place was not set at the correct time. He was told that this was because the electricity had been off during the exercise just as it would have been in a real emergency. While we had a valid explanation, this incident showed us just how observant the examiners were.

Turkey Point's Schedule B exam was very fast-paced. First one department then another answered questions about what they did to improve quality. Generally we were able to put the employee who was most capable of giving good answers before the examiners, but not always. The examiners had their own ways of digging to the bottom of an issue, and it was a contest between us to see who would control the flow of the exam.

There was a young engineer at the plant who was responsible for preventive maintenance of the two emergency diesel generators. Because these generators are a very important part of the plant's safety system, they have to be extremely reliable and perform to very rigid standards. This particular engineer was good and told his story well, and we wanted him to get before an examiner. Just before he was to go on, he bent over to pick up some back-up material and split the rear seam of his brand-new pants. He insisted that he be allowed to make his presentation anyway. He was careful not to turn around before the examiners, and a couple of his fellow employees helped out by standing nearby to screen his backside from view. I laugh sometimes when I think of the job titles we could have invented for them! The young man gave an inspired presentation. All things considered, he probably had far more adrenaline than usual.

Then the Turkey Point exam was over. Their ability to cope with adversity had served them well. Our assessment that evening was that Turkey Point had passed. Now it was up to the rest of the company to do its part.

Wednesday, the third day, was set aside for the examiners to read over the material they'd been given and to compose their notes. Also they would have time to get together to plan the exam for the next two days and to travel to the next exam location. We concluded later that the rest must have done them a lot of good. They seemed to have become even stronger during the last two days. As time went on they were very much in control. Try as we might, they wouldn't let us sneak in any data for which they had not asked. Clearly, they were veterans and had been through all this before.

Day four would include the St. Lucie Nuclear Plant and the Ft. Myers Fossil Plant exams.

When I look back on the exam of the Ft. Myers plant, one thing stands out in my memory. A young technician in the plant's chemistry laboratory drew for her examiner a Ph.D. in chemistry who is also an expert in statistical quality control. The examiner started asking one question after another about a control system the technician used to regulate boiler water chemistry. He tested her with the most detailed questions and asked her questions with a false predicate to see whether she really understood or had just learned the answers by rote. He personally verified her mathematics. Then he asked her how she knew her instruments and data points were accurate. When she produced another control chart on how she did this, a new series of questions ensued. Overall, she answered questions nonstop for sixty minutes. A doctoral exam could not have been any more rigorous. When we studied her answers that evening, we did not find a single one that needed to be changed. It's my opinion that the examiner was intrigued by the fact that this technician was a woman and wanted to see just how good she was. While I have never asked him how he felt about that presentation, we thought she was great. She was another one of our early heroes.

For years the St. Lucie units have been some of the best-performing nuclear units. One or the other of them has ranked number one in the free world in performance three of the last five years. A few minutes into the St. Lucie exam, the chief examiner stopped the presenter, who was describing St. Lucie's success, and said, "Thank you, but we are not interested in that. What we want to see today is how your quality system works. We want to see how you implement the quality policies of top management." Thereafter, all the plant's plans and practice sessions went out the window. They followed the examiners' agenda for the duration. Again, we felt that our people did very well and that they had passed.

Friday was the final day for these two audit units. In the morning the two respective staff groups had their exams, and in the afternoon the units' closing general session was held.

I attended the closing session and made a few final remarks. The examiners seemed to be in the best mood of the whole week. In fact, some very kind remarks were made about us and our quality improvement progress in the power plant area.

When the examiners left to go back to Japan, we felt very good about the first week. But four weeks still remained before the exam was complete. And there were still four more units to be examined. We knew from experience that a lot of things can happen in four weeks.

The first thing that happened was a pep rally at the General Office. Our employees in the General Office were all fired up by what they had seen during the first week of the exam, but they had been mere bystanders. Their own exam was not until the end of the second week. They had so much energy stored up that they had to do something. So they staged a pep rally.

On their own, the various General Office departments organized skits. Then one afternoon they had the rally in the atrium of the General Office building. The skits were very funny and provided some welcome comic relief. One of the best was a group performing a rap song, with an interpreter translating the rap into Japanese!

When Marshall McDonald came to Florida Power & Light, he required everyone over sixty-five to retire, although he himself managed to stay on as chairman and CEO of FPL Group until he was seventy-two years old. By then even he had to admit that it was time to step down. Accordingly, in January 1989, Jim Broadhead had been chosen to be the new CEO of FPL Group. Coming from outside FPL, he was something of a surprise choice, but we were ready for a change.

Jim and I did not see each other very much for the first three or four months after his arrival, but as time went by we began to meet more often. Some of the meetings were strained and did not go well.

With about two weeks to go before the second week of the exam, Jim Broadhead and I had a meeting. It was not a happy one. We reached an agreement on four things: he was the boss; he and I were incompatible; I would retire at the end of January 1990, as of my sixty-second birthday; and my retirement plans would be announced immediately.

The news caught many people by surprise, not the least of whom were the examiners when I told them the news two weeks later. At least they knew before the prize was awarded that I would not be around personally to support the quality process at FPL.

In that same week, we got word that C.O. Woody, our executive vice president for power plants, had suffered a heart attack and was in the intensive care unit. While the power plants had already been examined, several large General Office departments that reported to C.O. had not. Of even more serious concern was the fact that he was scheduled to carry a major role during the corporate Schedule A exam and the general session at the end of the exam.

Fortunately, Joe Williams, a senior vice president, had been C.O.'s understudy and was familiar with his presentation. Joe began some rigorous practice sessions to polish his skills. There is nothing like being told you are part of the starting team to get a player to take the practice seriously. Indeed, Joe performed very well during the exam. C.O. himself probably would not have done much better.

On the other hand, C.O. was fit to be tied. He wanted to get out of the hospital and make his presentation anyway. Of course this was out of the question. So he insisted that he at least be allowed to follow what was happening on the videotapes. He later told me that not being able to take part in the exam was one of the big disappointments of his life. (By the way, he has fully recovered.)

There had been some big surprises in the last few weeks, but at least one occurrence was not a surprise: just as planned, the six Deming examiners arrived at FPL at 9:00 A.M. on August 14, 1989. The second week's schedule called for three of the five divisions—those responsible for activities that deal directly with customers—to be examined during the first two days. However, since this group of examiners included four who were seeing FPL for the first and only time, at the examiners' request half a day would also be spent at the power plants to give them a complete overview of the company.

As the second week began, the people at FPL were much more confident than they had been in the first week. Fear of the unknown was no longer a factor. The rest had done us good too.

One of the divisions' exams focused on customer complaints to the Florida Public Service Commission. When the examiners discovered that we had even received complaints from customers who had been caught stealing electricity, they just shook their heads. "You mean," they asked, "they are angry because they have been forced to stop stealing?" When we answered "Yes," they looked at each other. Sometimes America must seem very strange to the Japanese.

Since the exam schedules had been agreed on for over a month, we thought we understood which district offices would be examined. When the examiners arrived at the Western Division saying that they would select and announce which two of the five districts in that division would be examined, pure panic ensued. The division vice president's face was white as a sheet. He wasn't so worried about any district's ability to take the audit, but he could envision all of the physical and travel arrangements having to be redone instantly. As it turned out, the examiners announced the schedule just as planned and everything went ahead on schedule.

During the Southern Division audit, one of our first-line supervisors drew the same examiner who had grilled the lab technician at the Ft. Myers Plant. He underwent the same type of intense questioning on SQC tools and techniques. He did well, and he also received strong back-up support from his colleagues. In the three weeks between exams we had not been idle. Our people had used the extra time to study the questions and answers from the first week. In this instance it paid off. This is but one more example of how the pressure of the exam causes you to put out effort like nothing else.

Most of the examiners are authors of books on some aspect of quality. We had issued instructions that our people not ask the examiners to autograph copies of their books. Later we learned that a few did so anyway; however, the books were so used and dog-eared that it didn't do any harm, and may have even made a good impression.

When Tuesday afternoon came, the examiners went to three of the power plants. At each one they wanted to see a QIP team presentation. It was a chance for some of the union employees to show their QI stories, and the examiners got a chance to see some good ones. Our union employees were doing their part with distinction.

Something else was taking place; our employees were experiencing emotional highs and lows as they went through the exam. All the effort that had been so much a part of their life for the last few years was coming to an end. This made them sad. But it was ending well, and that had them on cloud nine. After the exam for each division was over, the people would go somewhere and celebrate, bittersweet celebrations akin to graduations: you know that things have changed and will never be the same again.

One such celebration began a little too early. Our presentations had adhered to the schedule almost to the second, but in one case the goodbyes and some picture taking took an extra ten minutes. Just as the examiners were about to leave, a roar and cheering came from the exam support room staff, who thought the examiners had left. It was very audible to the examiners and we didn't know what to say. The examiners quickly relieved the moment's tension by smiling and clapping themselves.

The examiners had scheduled Wednesday as a catch-up, planning, and rest day. Then on Thursday the corporate Schedule A exam began, during which five of the top management made our presentations. We had learned our lessons and it seemed to go well. Again, it went by very fast.

We had set up a television monitor with which we could send little messages to the person at the lectern. The only cue I recall receiving was the instruction to *SMILE.*

Then it was time for all of the twenty-one departments of the General Office to put on their Schedule B audits. Three rooms were in continuous use with two examiners in each one. We alternated among six rooms overall; as one department finished, the examiners moved to the room next door. Immediately thereafter the old room was cleared and another department came in and set up for its exam. We were as busy as a three-ring circus.

This pace continued until Friday afternoon, when the General Office general session was held, followed by a one-hour executive session. I won't say much about the executive session since we were told not to talk about the matters discussed, except that the company had seven people present and all of them took part in the discussions.

The farewells were formal but friendly, and the examination was over. Some of our people told me that there was going to be a celebration at the end of the examination at one of the local hotels. They asked me please to join in. I could tell that it was going to be a good party even before I got there. As I walked from the lobby of the hotel to the ballroom I was getting kisses from the ladies and high fives from the men, and I could hear the band playing a Latin beat.

# The Deming Prize Award

We would hear whether or not we had won on October 23. Everyone who for one reason or another was to be out of the office that day had left instructions on how they could be reached with the news.

While it had been two months since the exam was completed, the examiners had not been idle. They had organized their own notes and met as pairs to agree on the scores for each of the units examined. Then the entire audit team had met and put together the overall score for the company. Over the weekend of October 21–22, the entire Deming Prize committee had met and heard reports on each of the companies that had been examined in 1989. Finally they decided, as a group, who had won and who would have to try again. Note that they don't declare anyone a loser; they just say that you must keep trying to improve.

One of the principal benefits of the audit is the report a company receives after the exam. The examiners put a great deal of effort and thought into their reports, and they provide valuable insight for further improvement activities.

We had given some thought to how we would publicize the news if we won. At one time we considered a rather elaborate advertising plan. However, since we had said all along that the principal purpose of going for the prize was customer satisfaction and not our own collective ego, this idea was scrapped. Ours would be a reactive mode. We would put out a small press release and then respond to questions from the media. As I look back, I think that this was a bad decision. Our people worked very hard for a long time. Most of them put in many extra hours without pay. They earned the right to a loud public pat on the back.

Wayne Brunetti received the call at his home about 3:30 in the morning on October 23. We had been awarded the Deming Application Prize for 1989! In all, there would also be nine other winners in 1989. This was the largest number of winners in many years. All of the others were Japanese companies. We were, and as of this writing still are, the only company outside Japan to win the Deming Application Prize.

The news caused a sense of deep satisfaction throughout the company. In truth, it was only confirmation of what everyone thought would happen, but then you never know. Now it was official and it would be ours forever. We had done it. But the news also saddened us in a way, for it meant the end of the quest that had occupied so much of our time and emotions over the last four years.

Then the letters and faxes started coming. At first just a few. The Japanese companies feel that it shows they are on top of events if they are first, and their congratulations were among the earliest. But more kept arriving day after day, hundreds of them, and most of the ones that came to me were signed by the president or chairman. Apparently half of the Fortune 500 CEOs must have known we were going for the Deming Prize. In addition to these CEOs, many people that I had not heard from in years sent me some very nice letters too. I was also very pleased when the

Miami Chamber of Commerce ran a full-page letter of congratulations to the company and its employees. At least the Chamber gave them a pat on the back.

The news prompted the media to call. The local newspapers were the first to show up at our door. Most of them didn't even know what the Deming Prize was. We tried our best to talk about quality improvement and customer satisfaction but all they wanted to know about was how much it cost and whether the ratepayers were expected to pay for our ego trip. In truth there is no way to calculate a precise cost. The practice sessions helped us understand how to improve quality in general and how to win customer satisfaction. How are these to be estimated in terms of cost? The improvements to the meeting rooms, and other benefits, continue to be useful. However, someone did finally come up with a ballpark figure of $1.5 million.

When the local newspapers came out the next morning, that was the way most of the stories were written: FPL spends $1.5 million to win some esoteric prize. Near the end of the items were a few words about quality improvement. On the other hand, the national newspapers and wire services carried much more favorable stories. Sometimes you lose, sometimes you win, sometimes you are rained out.

The magazine accounts of our having won the Deming Prize focused much more on the importance of the quality improvement results we had obtained. They understood and appreciated the rigorous process that had to be learned and applied before we could win. And at least one magazine didn't have much respect for the early and negative newspaper stories, calling them "churlish." Thank you, *Forbes.*

The award ceremonies were to take place in Tokyo on November 13 and 14 as part of a two-day conference for top management on TQC. Before then there was still some work to be done. A document describing the TQC process of each of the ten winning companies would be handed out at the ceremonies. In our case, this meant preparing a thirty-page summary of our description of QIP. Of course, we had most of the material at hand but it had to be summarized, updated, and then translated into Japanese and delivered to JUSE.

The award ceremonies themselves, the last part of the first day of the conference, were held in Keidanren Hall in downtown Tokyo. Attendance was by invitation only and was limited to about 400. Just before the actual awards, the CEO of Fuji-Xerox, Mr. T. Kobayashi, delivered a keynote address on the globalization of industry and markets. I know Mr. Kobayashi well, and I found his remarks very much in accord with my own views. He is a good representative of the modern Japanese industrialist.

Opening remarks were made about the 1989 Deming Prize winners by the president of JUSE, Kohei Suzue, and then a prize was given to a representative from each company. I had the honor of receiving the prize for FPL, and was given the courtesy of making a few remarks. Those receiving the prize before me looked very serious when they were on the dais. I tried my best to put on my deadpan face but it didn't work. My emotions took over and I have to confess that a huge smile broke out on my face. I hope that the Japanese were able to forgive my lack of stoicism.

Picture taking and a news conference ensued. About fifty reporters covered the awards. Needless to say, I stood out in several ways and therefore was asked a lot of questions. All of the subsequent reports I read in Japan were very positive toward FPL; I never read even a hint that the award should have remained exclusively Japanese.

The awards ceremony was followed by a reception for all those who had attended the ceremonies, as well as many others. I don't remember much about the reception; it is a blur of shaking hands, answering questions, and bowing. It reminded me of my daughter's wedding reception.

On the next day, November 14, there was an all-day lecture series at the Hibiya Hall, a very large hall seating over 2,000 people. The schedule called for each of the winning companies to spend about twenty-five minutes describing its quality improvement story. Again, I was the spokesman for FPL. When we arrived, at what I thought was an early hour, we found a double line of people two blocks long waiting to get in. As we entered the hall we were handed an inch-thick document containing the written description of all the winners' TQC processes. Included, of course, was the one we had sent to JUSE a month before, but since it was in Japanese I couldn't read it.

The nature of the presentations varied somewhat. Some of them were very detailed and used a lot of data. I chose to make a much more general address. Our written report contained the detailed information, and moreover, as the first overseas winner I felt that my address should encompass the bigger picture. I tried to make the point that total quality management was very rapidly spreading around the world. (The full text of my speech can be found in the appendix.) Then it was all over and we walked out into a beautiful fall day in Tokyo.

I am constantly asked, "What does FPL do to keep up the momentum? Will FPL continue to improve quality? Is FPL going to slacken its efforts and regress?" Only time will tell the answer to these questions. But I can say that many people want to see FPL continue in the forefront of quality improvement, and that makes me very optimistic.

# The Malcolm Baldrige National Quality Award: A Brief Legislative History

*F*ew things in the last three years have had as great an impact on the way American management views itself as the Malcolm Baldrige Award. Literally thousands of companies are using the criteria of the Baldrige Award judging process to evaluate their quality improvement management systems. The award and its winners are being recognized all over the world as representatives of world-class quality.

How did this come to happen? Since I was deeply involved in the legislative process that created the Malcolm Baldrige National Quality Award, I think it desirable to describe what happened for the historical record.

There were several early attempts to create a national quality award in America. A number of different organizations had attempted to set up their own version of the Japanese Deming Application Prize for quality. Even though a lot of work had been done, nothing had yet achieved what their authors had planned. Much of the thought that went into these early efforts, however, was used in the creation of the Malcolm Baldrige Award, and this greatly accelerated the implementation of the award.

In the summer of 1985, after we had made several trips to Japan, some of us at FPL were talking about what we had seen. The course of the conversation turned to American business practices. Since we were well aware of the Deming Prize and its effect on Japanese management, someone said it would be nice if we had a similar prize in the United States. Before I had really thought about what I was saying, I heard myself promising to see what I could do about it.

I knew that there were categories of the Deming Prize for large and small companies as well as for divisions or even plants of companies. I knew that the winners had to undergo a rigorous exam and that the winning companies could advertise their success. Finally, I knew that the award ceremony was a big, big affair.

With that limited knowledge, I considered what an American quality award should be and what we could borrow from the Deming Prize process.

For an award to have the most prestige and stand for world-class quality, it seemed that several things would be desirable. For the greatest visibility, the award should be made by the president of the United States. Also, the number of winners should be strictly limited. The Deming Prize is awarded to an average of about six companies per year. I think that many people in America tend to think more is better, but this is not always true. I remembered the old Army/Navy E of World War II. This was an award given by the government to those companies that made an extraordinary effort in supporting the war effort. In the beginning they were few in number and very prestigious but as the war came to its end, so many were given out that they didn't mean very much anymore. They were like Cracker Jack prizes. This was acceptable in this case because the war was ending and the award had served its purpose. But in the competitive battles for quality, there is no end. It therefore seemed to me that the quality award should be strictly limited in number if it was to have maximum prestige. And I felt that the winners should be able to advertise that they had won, as the Japanese did. With those simple concepts in mind, I began to think about how to bring such an award system into being.

Because a large percentage of proposed federal legislation has an impact on the electric power industry, and we in the industry are forced to keep up with proceedings in Congress, the industry has a number of very able Washington legislative representatives. Florida Power & Light has one of the best in Richard Sewell. When I talked with him about my idea for an American quality award and how to get the federal government interested in quality, he suggested that I speak to Congressman Don Fuqua. At the time Mr. Fuqua was Chairman of the House Science, Space, and Technology Committee. He was also a Floridian whom I had known for years.

One of the things I learned in my discussions with Congressman Fuqua in 1985 was that some members of the Science, Space, and Technology Committee were planning a fact-finding mission to Asia. The plan was to visit several Asian countries, including Japan, during the August recess. I asked Don Fuqua if, while they were in Japan, it would be possible to include a presentation for the committee on the Japanese quality management system and the Deming Prize. The answer was "yes" and the arrangements were made. Then Don's wife, Nancy, got very sick and the trip was abruptly canceled.

Around the first of December 1985, I got a call from Jim Turner, the executive director of the staff of the Science, Space, and Technology Committee, saying that some of the committee members were going to Asia during the Christmas recess and that they had expressed an interest in hearing the presentation on quality and the Deming Prize. Could I arrange it?

The period from Christmas until after the new year is a major holiday period in Japan. We tried to get several of the most prominent experts on quality to come in from their holiday for a presentation, without any success. Finally Dr. Kano prevailed on Dr. Kaoru Ishikawa to make the presentation. It could not have worked out better, because Dr. Ishikawa was one of the original four leaders in the quality movement in Japan and the author of many books on the subject.

Our QIP director, Kent Sterett, handled the arrangements. This was the first time we were involved in this kind of activity; even the U.S. Embassy was taking an active role. We had come a long way from just being an electric utility company in Florida. The meeting took place as planned and, as expected, Dr. Ishikawa covered the subject matter very well. The audience's awareness about quality and its importance was significantly improved.

Upon our return to the United States, Jim Turner began to draft some proposed legislation to create a national quality award. We were pleased to be asked for our ideas on the subject. Hearings were held in 1986 and Dr. Juran, Doug Ekings (who was chairman of the American Society for Quality Control at the time), and I testified for the bill.

About this time I heard through Richard Sewell that the Commerce Department had been considering its position on the proposed national quality award and tentatively decided to oppose the bill. I was able to discover some of their concerns and arrange for a meeting with the people at Commerce. As we discussed the bill we were able to agree to the changes they wanted, or in some cases, convince them that there wasn't a serious problem with the language in the bill.

They wanted, for example, the secretary of Commerce as well

as the president to be able to make the awards. They also wanted the secretary to be able to add government agencies to the list of categories for the award. On the other hand, they dropped their concern about the winners being able to advertise the fact. All of their concerns were successfully addressed, and when the meeting ended, the Commerce Department agreed to support the bill. From that meeting forward Malcolm Baldrige and the Commerce Department wholeheartedly endorsed and supported the legislation to create a national quality award. The bill did not call for the expenditure of tax monies; this is the era of Gramm-Rudman, after all. Rather, the private sector was to fund the award. Without this provision, I don't think the bill would ever have passed Congress. And yet, even with all this progress, there just wasn't enough time left in the 99th Congress to get the legislation passed.

As the 100th Congress began in 1987, Congressmen Walgren and Boehlert reintroduced the bill to create a national quality award. Hearings were expedited and set for early March. Again, I testified along with others for the bill and it passed out of the committee on May 13, picking up more and more sponsors as it went along. I was gratified that almost all of Florida's delegation were sponsors on the bill. Shortly thereafter the bill passed the full House.

Now it was time to turn to the Senate. I went back to Washington to see Senator Graham of Florida. We met for breakfast and I explained the bill and its purpose. He readily agreed to help. Richard Sewell also obtained the support of several other senators, including some important support from Senator Rockefeller of West Virginia. Various other senators were contacted by the Washington representatives of other electric utilities and asked to support the bill.

The bill moved through the Senate without much difficulty.

There was some opposition from an organization that subsequently became a full supporter of the quality award and shall therefore remain nameless. I think it was a case of "not invented here"; in any case, the opposition came too late to do much damage. As the *Washington Post* observed when it commented on the bill to create the award, this is the kind of legislation that the Senate loves to pass.

The bill had passed out of the committee when Malcolm Baldrige had an unfortunate rodeo accident. The full Senate added his name to the award and passed the bill out on the day of his funeral. President Reagan signed it into law with little delay.

Late in 1987 the president formally announced the Malcolm Baldrige National Quality Award during a ceremony at the White House. At that time he announced that he wanted to make the first awards in 1988. I was very pleased when I was called upon to make a few remarks about the award on this occasion.

On that occasion the new secretary of Commerce, William Verity, told me that he had a strong commitment to quality and that he was personally going to work hard to make the award a success from the very start. I think that a significant factor in the almost overnight success of the award was the strong leadership of both the president and the secretary of Commerce.

One day not long after the bill had been signed into law, I got a call from Curt Reimann of the National Bureau of Standards (now the National Institute of Standards and Technology—NIST). Reimann pointed out that the bureau had been given the job of organizing the award process on a tight schedule, but no money or other resources had been provided. Since he felt that I was one of the principal architects, he suggested that I help out with the solution. I saw his point.

One of the most pressing needs was for somebody to help work with all the outside groups involved in quality improvement to consider their ideas on implementation. And then there were a million administrative matters to manage. We had the perfect man for the job at FPL. Alan Siebe was just completing a one-year stint as a presidential executive exchange participant. He had worked at the Commerce Department and he even still had his identification badge. So he returned for what was supposed to be six more months—it turned out to be nine.

Two new groups were formed. A Board of Overseers made up of prominent members of the American quality community was to help the Department of Commerce formulate the policies for the award process. A Board of Examiners was chosen to manage the judging process. In addition, a contractor was selected to take over many of the day-to-day tasks that needed to be performed. The contractor chosen was one made up of a consortium of the American Society for Quality Control (ASQC) and the American Productivity and Quality Center (APQC). All together, these groups and the bureau did a truly Herculean job of putting together the entire structure for the award in only six months' time.

But there was still another task outstanding—obtaining the money to pay for it all. That was where I felt I personally could be most helpful. About six CEOs had pledged financial support for one of the earlier quality prize attempts. One of them was Sandy McDonnell, CEO of McDonnell Douglas Corporation. I called Sandy and got his agreement to help raise $6.6 million. He took about half of the Fortune 100 and I took the other half. We eliminated those companies we thought would have no interest in quality, i.e., those companies that had either no reputation or a poor reputation for quality. We may have judged some of them wrongly, and a few of those we omitted have since volunteered a contribution. You may be sure that my opinion about those companies has changed.

We were each left with about forty CEOs to call. The response we got was very encouraging. It was hard to catch the CEOs but once we caught them and told them what we wanted, almost all of them were happy to contribute to the fund. Only three turned me down, and I think Sandy's experience was about the same. We didn't want a lot of money from any one company because we wanted the support to come from the entire spectrum of American industry. And then, before funds could be accepted, a foundation had to be set up and tax-exempt status obtained for it.

About halfway through our fund-raising efforts, we got a jolt. The National Bureau of Standards told us that the estimated budget had gone up and that we needed to raise at least $10 million. I called Sandy and asked if he would step up to the larger sum if I would. After a long pause, he said yes. Ultimately we were able to raise even more than that amount as word about the quality award got around and others wanted to be part of the effort.

We also wanted to keep the funding of the foundation separated as far as possible from the judging process. Of course, there will always be some who will say that the two go together, but we didn't want such a charge to have any grounds at all. In fact, the judges are never told who has given what to the foundation.

In 1988 Sandy became the first president of the foundation and I followed him the second year. John Young, CEO of Hewlett-Packard, was the third president and John Marous of Westinghouse followed in 1991.

I am sometimes asked why FPL didn't go for the Malcolm Baldrige Award. There are two reasons. First, we were implementing a Japanese-style management system and were well on our way toward the Deming challenge when the Malcolm Baldrige Award came into being. To change in midstream would have been confusing, and there was no way we could do both at the same time.

Second, since FPL and I were so closely associated with the creation and funding of the Malcolm Baldrige Award, I was sure that if we won, it would be said that this was the reason. That would not have been good for FPL or the award. We had put too much effort into the award to do anything that would harm it.

Originally I thought that it would take at least two years to put everything in place, but it was done in less than one year. In large part this was possible because the entire professional quality community, the National Bureau of Standards, and the American business community pitched in and made it happen. It was a national effort of the finest type and a good example of what Americans can do when they make up their minds.

Just as he had said he wanted to do, President Reagan made the first awards at the White House in November of 1988. Motorola Corporation and Westinghouse Nuclear Fuel were the first large companies awarded the award. Most of us felt that the judges had done well and set high standards for the future winners. The second year's winners, Xerox and Milliken, were also world class in their quality results and processes and, if anything, brought the standards for the 1990 winners—Cadillac, Federal Express, IBM Rochester, and Wallace—even higher.

It seems to me that the quality award has come very far indeed in just a few years. I am afraid that its biggest problem now might be its own success. There will clearly be attempts to increase the number of awards, just like the Army/Navy E. To maintain the prestige of the award, I hope that this will not happen.

Dozens of CEOs have told their people they will win the Malcolm Baldrige Award by 1991 or 1992. Obviously, not all of them are going to be able to win that soon, and there are going to be a lot of disappointed and frustrated CEOs.

Nevertheless, the Malcolm Baldrige National Quality Award has focused attention on quality improvement in a way that nothing else could have done. It will not be the answer to all of America's problems, but it will be a big part of the answer to improving America's competitiveness in the world marketplace. It has truly become a national prize. Many, many people have contributed to its success and I am proud to have played my part.

# The Future

$S$o what? Will anything truly profound result from all of this quality improvement effort in America? I am convinced that the results have already been profound. The number of companies making breakthroughs in world-class quality is growing daily. More and more managements are becoming aware that slogans and strongly worded letters on quality alone are not going to get the job done. They now see that they need a systematic way to manage for quality, and they have started their companies with determination on the long journey to quality and greater customer satisfaction.

The Malcolm Baldrige Award will continue to be the polestar of American quality. As more and more Baldrige winners emerge as role models, it will be harder and harder for the nonbelievers to avoid the truth. As the winning companies prosper and gain market share, Wall Street will also come to understand and respect total quality management. Already I know of one investment firm that invests exclusively in companies that use TQM; surely there are, and will be, others.

The European community is developing its own award for quality, patterned after the Deming Prize and the Malcolm Baldrige Award. There is a rapidly growing appreciation among the better European companies that they must make major changes in quality if they are to remain competitive and strong in the new marketplace. They view quality as the way to survive. A number of good practitioners exist in Germany, Sweden, and the United Kingdom at this time.

Australia and the nations of Southeast Asia are also making progress toward improved quality. Some of my former colleagues are counseling a growing number of Australian companies on how to manage for quality. Japanese counselors are to be found teaching quality management all over Singapore, Thailand, and Indonesia.

The movement is truly worldwide; the number of companies using TQM to improve quality is so large and the momentum so great that managements who ignore it run a grave risk regarding the future of their companies.

Every American company in the Fortune 500 is going to have a competitor that is using TQM. Look out, they are after your customers! If you are in international markets you are living in the same environment except more so. To slightly misquote Satchel Paige, "If you look back you will see someone gaining on you."

What must you do? What should you do first? If you are in top management, start to gather all the information you can about your customers and what they want. Obtain accurate data from your customers on how you are doing in meeting those wants. Get data from the customers you would like to have or have lost on why they didn't choose to buy from you. Get data on how well the competition is doing. Areas that need to be improved will quickly become obvious. Set a few dramatic improvement goals.

In parallel with this data-gathering effort, begin to find out all you can about TQM. Visit companies that have a good reputation for quality and see how they got there. And finally, begin to install your own TQM process. Accept the fact that it is going to take time and effort. A word of caution is in order—every management consultant in America has added the word quality to his or her portfolio and will profess great skills and ability to teach the process. Many of them will do more harm than good because they are incompetent. So beware.

However, when you make a mistake—and you will—don't get discouraged and stop. Learn a lesson, or as we say, PDCA the process and do better the next time. You are dealing with a critical success factor that may even be a survival issue for your company.

If you are in middle management in a company that is not using TQM, you need to learn about TQM and then talk to top management about it. Urge them to learn about it. Often top management is slow to change because they anticipate resistance from the rest of the company. When they see that this is not as great a problem as they thought, they are more willing to make the change. It doesn't always work that way, but I know of several very good companies that got started from a bottom-up push.

As I said in the very beginning of this book, there are three most important factors for successful TQM. First is a strong, visible, and consistent commitment by top management. This needs to be constantly emphasized and reinforced as a key success factor for the company. Second is a strong commitment to education and training of all employees. And last, it must be profoundly understood that there has to be a concrete system in place to make it happen, a systematic way of encouraging all employees to do their best. To this recipe for success I would add a dash of patience and a teaspoon of perseverance. Good luck!

# *Appendix:*
# *John J. Hudiburg Address at Deming Presentation, November 14, 1989*

*T*hank you. Once again I extend my deep appreciation to the members of JUSE for both the opportunity and the honor of being named the first overseas winner of the Deming Prize.

I will deliver my address in English, which will be translated by FPL's interpreter, Noriko Hosoyamada. I suppose that this is the first time that such a presentation has been made in English. It's my strong wish that in the future many other prize winners will also have a need for interpreters and in many different languages.

I will briefly describe our company's quality management system. However, I believe the unique circumstances of being the first overseas company to win the Deming Prize call for at least some comments of a more general nature.

First of all, the news that FPL had been named a Deming Prize winner created a great deal of attention in the United States. The news has appeared in numerous publications and on television stations throughout our country. Appropriately, in most instances the focus was not on FPL, but rather on the quality improvement process itself.

Also, I can assure you that the significance of an American company receiving this prestigious recognition in Japan *has* been noticed by the leaders of our country, and the importance of what JUSE has done in establishing the overseas prize has not been overlooked.

Last week, I was present in Washington, D.C., where our nation's Malcolm Baldrige Quality Awards were presented by President Bush. While I was there, I received congratulations from both the president and the secretary of Commerce for our Deming achievement.

I'm sometimes asked why FPL chose to pursue the Deming Prize rather than our own country's quality award. There were several reasons for our doing so.

It has been, since 1985, our desire to install a *Japanese* style quality management system. This goal was set long before the Baldrige Awards were created.

The principal purpose of our Deming challenge was to inspire and motivate all of our employees, including myself, to work very hard to learn and practice a Japanese TQC management system.

I felt the Deming challenge was the most effective way to further this goal. Moreover, I felt it would have caused confusion to shift from Deming to Baldrige in mid-course.

I must tell you that our expectations were fully met. Our people worked very hard and our progress has been far greater during 1989 than in any prior year.

Now a little about our company. I'm sure that some of you may not be familiar with Florida Power & Light.

We are an electric utility company that provides electricity to about half the state of Florida, which is located in the southeast corner of the United States. We have 15,000 employees, and with more than three million customers we're the fourth largest and the fastest growing electric utility in our country.

Our operating revenues for the last twelve months were just under $5 billion and the total assets of our company are well over $11 billion.

Because FPL as an electric company is considered a natural monopoly, I'm often asked why we're so interested in the quality improvement process. People seem to assume that manufacturing companies engaged in competition for market share would be interested in total quality control, but electric utilities would *not* be.

My response is that we've found that the problems we must cope with can be managed through TQC better than any other way.

Also, our future corporate health depends on continuing customer satisfaction, which can best be realized through TQC.

Finally, our management and our employees take a great deal of pride in what they do and they want to be the best in the utility industry. To accomplish this, they need TQC. In other words, we use TQC for the same reason any other company does.

During the 1970s, we experienced a great many problems at FPL. Inflation, the OPEC oil embargo, and the nuclear accident at Three Mile Island were just a few of the factors that led to tremendous customer dissatisfaction with FPL.

Fortunately, our search for a management system to help us effectively deal with our problems brought us to Japan.

In 1984, we visited a number of very fine Japanese companies and we were introduced to TQC. I readily admit that we didn't understand how it was being done, but we *did* understand the results.

And then, with assistance from our friends at Kansai Electric Company, we began to learn about TQC bit by bit. In 1985, Kansai introduced us to Dr. Asaka and our other counselors, and whatever success we've had is due to their teaching. We owe them many thanks.

With their help, we expanded our quality improvement efforts from quality teams to policy deployment, quality in daily work, vendor quality, and so on.

The methods we used are the same as those followed in Japan.

The principles of our program, for example, focus on customer satisfaction, management by fact, the PDCA cycle, and respect for people. Also, the amount of time taken at FPL to learn the system was probably very similar to the Japanese experience.

In addition, the results obtained as we began to improve and integrate the elements of our quality system were very typical of those seen by Japanese companies.

For example, we saw customer complaints reduced to their lowest level of the last ten years, and our customer surveys revealed that the percentage of satisfied customers was climbing sharply.

We improved reliability 57 percent. We saw employee lost-time injuries drop 65 percent. And while these and many other improvements were taking place, we have made major reductions in the price of electricity.

We have also experienced many intangible effects. These include a renewed sense of pride and respect among employees, and a new way of focusing on customer satisfaction.

The Deming challenge was something that no one in our company will ever forget. And last August, when the eight JUSE examiners visited with us, was one of the most exciting times in the history of FPL.

As we anxiously awaited word from your country about the Deming Prize, we took time to reflect on what we had done, but even more importantly, we took time to reflect on what remained to be done. We concluded that when it comes to quality improvement, we have much work left to do. It is the recognition of the need for continued improvement that is our greatest lesson learned.

With just a few minutes remaining in the Deming examination, Dr. Kume asked, "Mr. Hudiburg, what advice would you give to a chief executive considering the implementation of TQC?"

I replied that I would emphasize three points.

First, top management must be *totally* committed. Secondly, management must be prepared to support education and training in TQC on a very large scale and over a long period of time.

Finally, to gain the full benefit of a quality improvement program, it *must* be implemented in a complete, companywide system.

We have, I believe, demonstrated our commitment to quality at FPL in all those respects.

I know that all those who draw on the TQC system to improve the way they do business are expected to give something back—to add value to the quality process.

Our major contribution, I believe, is simply this:

We have shown, in a very narrow sense, that the Japanese management system can work for an American utility company.

We installed the system just as we were taught by our counselors. Despite the problems of language and distance, I'm convinced that our experience is identical to what one would see in a Japanese company our size.

Therefore, in a much broader sense, however, we have shown that the Japanese management system can work for *any kind* of company, *any place* in the world.

I believe there is a global significance to what we have been allowed to achieve. And again I thank JUSE for having the foresight to allow us to share in the Deming experience. JUSE is in the forefront of those who are working for the well-being of all mankind and that is a nice place to be.

Thank you.

# Recommended Readings

Amsden, Robert T., Howard E. Butler, and Davida M. Amsden. *SPC Simplified: Practical Steps to Quality.* White Plains, NY: Quality Resources, 1986.

Aubrey, Charles A., II, and Patricia K. Felkins. *Teamwork: Involving People in Quality and Productivity Improvement.* White Plains, NY: Quality Resources; and Milwaukee, WI: ASQC Quality Press, 1988.

Camp, Robert C. *Benchmarking: The Search for Industry Best Practices That Lead to Superior Performance.* White Plains, NY: Quality Resources; and Milwaukee, WI: ASQC Quality Press, 1989.

Crosby, Philip B. *Quality Is Free: the Art of Making Quality Free.* New York: McGraw-Hill, 1979.

Deming, W. Edwards. *Out of the Crisis.* Cambridge, MA: MIT Center for Advanced Engineering Study, 1986.

Feigenbaum, Armand V. *Total Quality Control,* 3rd ed. New York: McGraw-Hill, 1983.

Fukuda, Ryuji. *Managerial Engineering: Techniques for Improving Quality and Productivity in the Workplace,* rev. ed. David Perlstein, ed. Noriko Hosoyamada, trans. Cambridge, MA: Productivity Press, 1986.

Imai, Masaaki. *Kaizen: The Key to Japan's Competitive Success.* New York: Random, 1986.

Ishikawa, Kaoru. *Guide to Quality Control,* 2nd ed. Tokyo: Asian Productivity Organization, 1986.

Ishikawa, Kaoru. *Introduction to Quality Control.* Tokyo: 3A Corporation, 1990.

Ishikawa, Kaoru. *What Is Total Quality Control? The Japanese Way.* Englewood Cliffs, NJ: Prentice-Hall, 1985.

Juran, J.M. *Juran's Quality Control Handbook,* 4th ed. New York: McGraw-Hill, 1988.

King, Bob. *Better Designs in Half the Time: Implementing QFD Quality Function Deployment in America.* Methuen, MA: GOAL/QPC, 1987.

Kume, Hitoshi. *Statistical Methods for Quality Improvement.* Tokyo: The Association for Overseas Technical Scholarship, 1985.

Mizuno, Shigeru. *Company-Wide Total Quality Control.* Tokyo: Asian Productivity Organization, 1988.

Mizuno, Shigeru. *Management for Quality Improvement: The Seven New QC Tools.* Cambridge, MA: Productivity Press, 1988.

*Quality Function Deployment: A Collection of Presentations and QFD Case Studies.* American Supplier Institute.

Rosander, A.C., *The Quest for Quality in Services.* White Plains, NY: Quality Resources; and Milwaukee, WI: ASQC Quality Press, 1989.

# *Index*